Leadership
KEY CNCEPTS

Leadership
KEY C NCEPTS

Unlock Your Path to Extraordinary Leadership:
21 Key Skills and Principles for Unleashing Your Full Potential

Roger C. Edwards, Jr.

EDVARDSON CREATIVE

www.edvardsoncreative.com

Leadership Key Concepts

Unlock your Path to Extraordinary Leadership: 21 Key Skills & Principles for Quickly Unleashing Your Full Potential

ISBN: 979-8-218-24736-2 (Paperback)
ISBN: 979-8-218-24791-1 (ePub))

Library of Congress Control Number: 2023913965

EDVARDSON CREATIVE

Edvardson Creative, LLC

www.edvardsoncreative.com
www.leadershipkeyconcepts.com

"Everything begins with an idea."

- *Earl Nightingale*

Leadership
KEY CONCEPTS

You Are Here
Great Leadership Starts Right Where You Are

1

Calm Confidence
Leaders Know and They Know That They Know

2

Be at Your Best Regardless
How You Do Anything is How You Do Everything

3

The Certain Way
Leaders Do Things in a Certain Way

4

The Common Denominator Of Success
Leaders Do What Failures Don't Like to Do

5

Thoughts Become Things
Leaders Think in Pictures and Attract Things to Them

6

Leadership
KEY CONCEPTS

You Are Here
Great Leadership Starts Right Where You Are

Introduction

Leadership is often associated with formal titles and positions of authority, creating the misconception that only a select few possess the ability to lead. However, true leadership goes far beyond these superficial markers. It is a mindset, a set of qualities, and a commitment to positive action that can be demonstrated by anyone, regardless of their current circumstances. You, as an individual, have the potential to be a leader and make a significant impact in your immediate environment. Let's explore how you can cultivate and demonstrate leadership qualities, contribute to personal growth, and become catalysts for positive change within your community and organization.

1. The Essence of Leadership

Leadership is a multifaceted concept that transcends formal titles and positions. It is not limited to those who hold positions of authority or power. Instead, great leadership is about the impact an individual can make and the influence they can have on others, regardless of their official position. Whether you are a student, an employee, a parent, or a community member, you have the potential to exhibit leadership qualities and make a meaningful difference in your surroundings.

Being a leader is about inspiring and guiding others towards common goals. It involves the ability to influence and motivate others to take action and achieve collective objectives. This influence can be exerted in various ways, such as through effective communication, leading by example, and building relationships based on trust and respect.

In a classroom setting, for example, a student can demonstrate leadership by actively participating in discussions, sharing ideas, and encouraging their peers to engage in collaborative learning. They can take the initiative to organize study groups, support classmates who are struggling, and contribute to a positive and inclusive learning environment.

Similarly, within the workplace, effective leadership can be displayed by team members at all levels. It involves taking ownership of one's work, displaying a strong work ethic, and inspiring colleagues through quality performance and a positive attitude. Leaders in the workplace go beyond their assigned tasks and take the initiative to identify areas for improvement, propose innovative solutions, and contribute to the overall success of the team or organization.

Parents also have the opportunity to demonstrate leadership within their families. They can create a nurturing and supportive environment, lead by example in terms of values and behaviors, and empower their children to develop their own leadership skills. By encouraging their children to take responsibility, make decisions, and contribute to the family's well-being, parents foster a sense of empowerment and personal growth.

Community members can exhibit leadership by actively engaging in their local communities. This can involve volunteering, participating in community initiatives, and advocating for positive change. By taking the initiative to address social, environmental, or economic issues, community leaders inspire others to get involved and make a difference.

KEY TAKEAWAY

Leadership extends far beyond formal titles and positions. It is not limited to those with authority, but rather it is a quality that can be demonstrated by individuals in any role or position. Leadership involves inspiring and guiding others towards shared goals, influencing positive change, and making a meaningful impact in one's surroundings. By embracing the opportunity to exhibit leadership qualities, regardless of official titles, individuals can contribute to a better future for themselves, their communities, and their organizations.

Key Qualities of Great Leaders

Great leaders possess a unique combination of qualities that enable them to excel in their roles and make a lasting impact. These key qualities not only set them apart but also contribute to their ability to inspire and motivate others. Let's explore some of the essential qualities that define great leaders:

1. Integrity: Integrity is truly the foundation of great leadership. Leaders with integrity demonstrate honesty, ethical behavior, and consistency in their actions. They align their words and deeds, earning the trust and respect of those around them. By acting with integrity, leaders inspire others to do the same and foster a culture of transparency and accountability.

2. Empathy: Empathy is the ability to understand and relate to the feelings and perspectives of others. Great leaders possess empathy, enabling them to connect with their team members on a deeper level. By demonstrating genuine care and understanding, leaders create an inclusive and supportive environment where individuals feel valued and motivated to contribute their best.

3. Vision: Vision is the ability to see beyond the present and envision a better future. Great leaders have a clear vision and can communicate it effectively to inspire others. Their vision provides a sense of purpose and direction, motivating individuals to work towards a shared goal. By articulating a compelling vision, leaders can rally their team and ignite a sense of passion and commitment.

4. Adaptability: In an ever-changing world, adaptability is crucial for effective leadership. Great leaders are flexible and open-minded, willing to embrace new ideas and approaches. They can navigate uncertainty and adjust their strategies when faced with challenges. By embracing change, leaders create a culture of resilience and empower their team members to embrace innovation and growth.

5. Resilience: Resilience is the ability to bounce back from setbacks and persevere in the face of adversity. Great leaders demonstrate resilience, maintaining a positive mindset and leading by example during challenging times. They inspire their team to stay focused, learn from failures, and find new opportunities for growth and success.

6. Effective Communication: Effective communication is essential for great leadership. Leaders who can articulate their ideas clearly and listen actively build strong relationships and foster collaboration. They create an environment where open and honest communication is valued, encouraging dialogue and understanding among team members.

7. Building Strong Relationships: Great leaders understand the power of building strong relationships. They invest time and effort in getting to know their team members, recognizing their strengths, and providing support and mentorship. By building trust and fostering positive relationships, leaders create a cohesive and motivated team.

These qualities work together to shape great leaders who inspire and motivate others, foster collaboration, and drive positive change. While individuals may naturally possess some of these qualities, they can also be developed and strengthened through self-reflection, learning, and practice. By cultivating these qualities, individuals can enhance their leadership abilities and make a significant impact in their organizations and communities.

2. Personal Leadership

Self-awareness and reflection are key elements of personal leadership. They involve gaining a deep understanding of oneself, including strengths, weaknesses, values, and passions. When individuals possess self-awareness, they can align their actions and behaviors with their core principles, enabling them to lead authentically and with integrity.

Self-awareness is a continuous process that involves introspection and reflection. It requires individuals to take the time to explore their thoughts, emotions, and motivations. By developing self-awareness, leaders can better understand their own biases, limitations, and areas for improvement.

Understanding your strengths is essential for personal leadership. By recognizing your unique talents and abilities, you can leverage them to contribute meaningfully and lead with confidence. Identifying strengths also allows leaders to delegate tasks effectively, fostering a collaborative environment where team members can thrive.

Equally important is an awareness of weaknesses. Recognizing areas for improvement enables leaders to seek development opportunities, whether through training, mentorship, or self-directed learning. By addressing weaknesses, leaders can enhance their skills and become more effective in their roles.

Values play a vital role in personal leadership. They act as guiding principles that shape decision-making and actions. Leaders who are in touch with their core values can make ethical choices and act with integrity. Aligning actions with values also promotes consistency, gaining the trust and respect of team members.

Passions drive motivation and energy. When leaders are aware of their passions, they can pursue meaningful work and inspire others with their enthusiasm. Passionate leaders demonstrate a genuine commitment to their goals, sparking excitement and dedication within their teams.

Self-reflection is also a crucial tool for personal growth and development. It involves regularly assessing your actions, decisions, and outcomes. By reflecting on successes and failures, leaders can gain valuable insights and learn from their experiences. This self-analysis allows for adjustments and improvements, leading to continuous growth as a leader.

Leadership styles can vary from person to person. Through self-awareness and reflection, individuals can identify their preferred leadership style and understand its impact on others. This insight allows leaders to adapt their approach to meet the needs of their team members and the situation at hand.

> *Self-awareness and reflection are essential components of personal leadership. By understanding strengths, weaknesses, values, and passions, individuals can lead authentically and with integrity. Through continuous self-analysis and development, leaders can enhance their effectiveness, inspire others, and foster a positive and inclusive work environment. Self-awareness and reflection serve as the foundation for personal growth and the cultivation of exceptional leadership skills.*

KEY TAKEAWAY

Taking Initiative and Embracing Ownership

Key elements of leadership are exercising initiative and accepting responsibility Great leaders are not passive bystanders; they actively seek opportunities, take responsibility, and drive positive change. Regardless of their position or title, individuals can exhibit leadership qualities by being proactive and making a difference in their spheres of influence.

Leadership requires individuals to step forward and take action. It involves identifying areas for improvement or opportunities for growth and taking the initiative to address them. Rather than waiting for someone else to initiate change, leaders seize the moment and actively work towards positive outcomes.

By taking ownership of their actions and their impact, leaders demonstrate accountability. They understand that their choices and decisions have consequences, both for themselves and for those around them. Leaders take responsibility for their actions, recognizing that they have the power to influence outcomes and make a meaningful difference.

Leadership also involves embracing challenges and setbacks. Great leaders understand that setbacks are an inherent part of the journey, but they don't let obstacles deter them. Instead, they approach challenges with a growth mindset and use them as opportunities for learning and improvement. Leaders persevere in the face of adversity, inspiring others with their resilience and determination.

Leaders also go above and beyond the tasks and obligations they are given. They actively seek opportunities to contribute beyond what is expected of them. They are proactive in identifying problems, proposing innovative solutions, and driving positive change. By demonstrating initiative, leaders inspire others to follow suit and create a culture of action and progress.

Leadership is not confined to those with formal authority. It is about taking ownership of one's sphere of influence, regardless of position or title. In any situation, individuals can demonstrate leadership by fostering collaboration, inspiring others, and driving positive outcomes.

By taking initiative, individuals become agents of change and catalysts for improvement. They create a ripple effect, motivating others to get involved and contribute to the greater good. Leadership is contagious, and by stepping forward, individuals can inspire a collective sense of ownership and responsibility.

KEY TAKEAWAY

Leadership begins with taking initiative and embracing ownership. It requires individuals to be proactive, identify opportunities, and take responsibility for their actions and impact. Regardless of position or title, anyone can demonstrate leadership by actively working towards positive change. Leadership is not limited to a select few; it is accessible to all who choose to step forward and make a difference.

Continuous Learning and Growth

Effective leadership requires constant learning and development. Leadership is not a static state but a dynamic process that requires individuals to constantly evolve and adapt. By actively seeking opportunities for personal development, expanding knowledge, acquiring new skills, and embracing feedback, leaders can enhance their abilities and remain effective in their roles.

Leaders who prioritize continuous learning understand that knowledge and skills are not finite but can be continually expanded upon. They seek out learning opportunities such as workshops, conferences, seminars, and online courses to gain new insights and stay abreast of emerging trends and best practices. By staying informed and up-to-date, leaders can make informed decisions and guide their teams more effectively.

A key component of continuing to grow is learning new abilities. Leaders actively identify areas for improvement and proactively seek opportunities to develop those skills. They invest time and effort into learning new technologies, enhancing communication and interpersonal skills, and honing their problem-solving and decision-making abilities. By continuously expanding their skill set, leaders become more versatile and better equipped to navigate complex challenges.

Feedback is an invaluable source of growth for leaders. They actively seek feedback from colleagues, superiors, and team members to gain insights into their strengths and areas for improvement. Feedback helps leaders understand how their actions impact others and provides opportunities for self-reflection and growth. By embracing feedback with an open mind and a willingness to learn, leaders can identify blind spots and make adjustments to their leadership style.

Leadership development programs and coaching are valuable resources for continuous learning and growth. These type of programs offer structured learning experiences and provide opportunities for leaders to explore new concepts, engage in self-reflection, and receive guidance from experienced professionals. By participating in such programs, leaders can gain fresh perspectives, enhance their self-awareness, and develop a deeper understanding of their leadership strengths and areas for development.

Adaptability is also fostered by ongoing learning and development. In today's fast-paced and ever-changing world, leaders must be able to navigate ambiguity and respond effectively to evolving circumstances. By staying curious, embracing new ideas, and being open to different perspectives, leaders can adapt their strategies and approaches to address emerging challenges.

KEY TAKEAWAY

Continuous learning and growth are integral to effective leadership. Leaders who prioritize personal development, expand their knowledge, acquire new skills, and embrace feedback are better equipped to navigate complex and changing environments. By remaining committed to their own growth, leaders inspire a culture of continuous learning within their teams and organizations. Leadership is a journey, and those who embrace lifelong learning will evolve, adapt, and make a positive impact on those they lead.

3. Leadership within Organizations

Within organizations, leadership is really about inspiring and influencing others. Great leaders understand that achieving shared objectives requires the active participation and commitment of their team members. By setting a compelling vision, communicating effectively, and fostering a supportive environment, leaders can motivate and empower their teams to achieve excellence.

One of the key responsibilities of a leader is to set a clear and compelling vision for the organization or team. A vision is a guiding statement that outlines the desired future state and serves as a source of inspiration. Leaders communicate this vision to their team members, helping them understand the purpose and direction of their collective efforts. A well-defined vision creates a sense of purpose and a shared understanding of the organization's goals, which is essential for aligning individual actions with the larger mission.

Effective communication influences and inspires others. Leaders must be able to convey their ideas, expectations, and vision clearly and compellingly. They use various communication channels to reach their team members, such as team meetings, emails, and one-on-one conversations. By being transparent and open in their communication, leaders foster trust and create an environment where team members feel informed and engaged.

In addition to setting a compelling vision and communicating effectively, leaders create a supportive environment that encourages collaboration and growth. They understand the importance of building strong relationships with their team members, fostering a culture of trust, respect, and psychological safety. Leaders actively listen to their team members, valuing their input and ideas, and providing feedback and guidance when necessary. By creating a supportive environment, leaders empower their team members to take risks, innovate, and contribute their best work.

The ability of leaders to inspire and motivate their staff is key. They recognize and celebrate the achievements of their team members, providing recognition and rewards for a job well done. Leaders also provide encouragement during challenging times, instilling confidence and resilience within the team. By serving as role models, leaders inspire their team members to reach their full potential and demonstrate the values and behaviors they expect from others.

Effective leaders also assign tasks and give their team members autonomy. They provide opportunities for growth and development, allowing individuals to take on new challenges and expand their skills. By trusting their team members and providing them with autonomy, leaders foster a sense of ownership and accountability, leading to increased motivation and engagement.

KEY
TAKEAWAY

Influencing and inspiring others is a crucial aspect of leadership within organizations. Great leaders set a compelling vision, communicate effectively, and foster a supportive environment. They motivate and empower their team members, creating a sense of purpose and engagement. By fostering collaboration, recognizing achievements, and providing opportunities for growth, leaders inspire their teams to achieve excellence and contribute to the shared objectives of the organization.

Building Relationships and Collaboration

Leadership requires cultivating relationships and encouraging teamwork. Great leaders understand that success is not achieved in isolation but through the collective efforts of a team. By actively listening, valuing diverse perspectives, and promoting a culture of inclusivity, leaders create an environment that encourages teamwork, innovation, and creativity.

One of the key aspects of building relationships is active listening. Leaders take the time to truly understand the thoughts, concerns, and ideas of their team members. They listen attentively, without judgment, and show genuine interest in what others have to say. By actively listening, leaders make their team members feel valued and respected, which in turn fosters trust and strengthens the relationship.

Valuing diverse perspectives is another important element of building relationships. Effective leaders recognize the unique strengths and experiences each team member brings to the table. They create an inclusive environment where everyone feels comfortable sharing their ideas and opinions, regardless of their background or position. By embracing diversity, leaders leverage the collective intelligence of the team and encourage innovative thinking.

Promoting a culture of inclusivity is key for building strong relationships and fostering collaboration. Leaders ensure that all team members feel welcomed, respected, and valued. They create a safe space where individuals feel free to express their thoughts and ideas, knowing that their contributions will be heard and considered. By promoting inclusivity, leaders encourage open communication and collaboration, leading to better problem-solving, increased creativity, and improved decision-making.

Trust may be the most important component of building relationships. Effective leaders establish trust by being reliable, consistent, and transparent in their actions and decisions. They follow through on their commitments and are honest in their communication. By fostering trust, leaders create an environment where team members feel comfortable taking risks, sharing their concerns, and working together towards common goals.

Building relationships and encouraging cooperation also need a high level of psychological safety. Leaders create an atmosphere where team members feel safe to express their thoughts and ideas without fear of judgment or retribution. They encourage constructive feedback and create a culture of learning and growth. By fostering psychological safety, leaders empower their team members to take risks, share diverse perspectives, and contribute their best work.

Building relationships and fostering collaboration are vital for effective leadership. By actively listening, valuing diverse perspectives, promoting inclusivity, and fostering trust and psychological safety, leaders create an environment where teamwork, innovation, and creativity thrive. By building strong relationships, leaders leverage the collective strengths of the team and inspire collaboration towards achieving shared goals. Effective leaders understand that successful outcomes are achieved through the power of collaboration and the synergy of a united team.

KEY TAKEAWAY

Mentoring and Developing Others

Mentoring and developing others is a key responsibility of great leaders. They understand that investing in the growth and development of their team members not only benefits the individuals but also contributes to the overall success of the organization. By providing guidance, mentorship, and opportunities for growth, leaders foster an environment that enables individuals to reach their full potential and contribute their best work.

One of the ways leaders support the development of their team members is through mentorship. They act as mentors, offering guidance, advice, and sharing their knowledge and experiences. By being accessible and approachable, leaders create a safe space for individuals to seek support and learn from their expertise. Mentoring helps individuals develop new skills, expand their perspectives, and navigate challenges more effectively.

Great leaders also provide opportunities for growth and development. They identify the strengths and interests of their team members and offer assignments, projects, or training programs that align with their aspirations. By providing these growth opportunities, leaders not only enhance the skills and knowledge of their team members but also demonstrate their belief in their potential.

Leaders encourage continuous learning and encourage their team members to acquire new skills and knowledge. They promote a culture of learning within the organization by encouraging participation in workshops, conferences, and seminars. By investing in the development of their team, leaders create a motivated and engaged workforce that is better equipped to adapt to changing circumstances and drive innovation.

In addition to formal development opportunities, leaders provide ongoing feedback and coaching. They provide regular performance feedback, highlighting areas of improvement and recognizing achievements. By offering constructive feedback, leaders help individuals identify their strengths and areas for growth, fostering a culture of continuous improvement.

A key component of mentoring and developing others is empowerment. Great leaders trust their team members to make decisions and take ownership of their work. They delegate responsibilities and provide support when needed, allowing individuals to take on new challenges and grow their skills. By empowering their team members, leaders inspire confidence, motivation, and a sense of ownership in the work they do.

Leaders create a supportive environment that values professional and personal growth. They encourage individuals to set goals and provide the necessary resources and support to achieve them. Great leaders recognize that personal development extends beyond professional skills and also support the well-being and work-life balance of their team members.

KEY TAKEAWAY

Mentoring and developing others is a critical aspect of great leadership. By providing guidance, mentorship, and opportunities for growth, leaders foster an environment that enables individuals to reach their full potential. They invest in the growth of their team members through mentorship, ongoing feedback, and providing growth opportunities. By empowering and supporting their team members' professional and personal development, leaders not only contribute to individual success but also create a motivated and engaged workforce that drives the success of the organization.

Leading Through Change

Change is inevitable in any organization or team, and great leaders understand the importance of navigating transitions and guiding their team members through them. By anticipating and embracing change, communicating the vision effectively, and inspiring resilience and adaptability, leaders create a sense of stability and inspire confidence during times of uncertainty.

Effective leaders anticipate change by staying informed and proactive. They keep an eye on industry trends, technological advancements, and shifts in the external environment that may impact their organization. By staying ahead of the curve, leaders can anticipate potential challenges and opportunities, allowing them to develop strategies and plans to navigate change effectively.

Communication is key when leading through change. Leaders must effectively communicate the vision, goals, and rationale behind the changes to their team members. By providing clear and transparent communication, leaders create a shared understanding of the change and its importance. They address concerns, answer questions, and provide ongoing updates to keep their team members informed and engaged.

During times of change, leaders play a critical role in inspiring resilience and adaptability. They acknowledge the challenges and uncertainties that come with change and help their team members navigate through them. By demonstrating their own resilience and adaptability, leaders inspire confidence and foster a culture of agility within their teams.

Great leaders provide support to their team members during transitions. They offer guidance, reassurance, and resources to help individuals navigate through change successfully. Leaders understand that change can be disruptive and may lead to resistance or fear. By actively listening and addressing concerns, leaders create a safe space for their team members to express their feelings and collaborate on finding solutions.

Leaders also help their team members see the opportunities that change presents. They highlight the potential for growth, learning, and innovation that can emerge from periods of transition. By framing change as a chance for personal and professional development, leaders inspire their team members to embrace new possibilities and explore creative solutions.

Leading through change is a critical aspect of effective leadership. By anticipating and embracing change, communicating the vision effectively, and inspiring resilience and adaptability, leaders create a sense of stability and inspire confidence during times of uncertainty. By providing support, resources, and guidance, leaders help their team members navigate through transitions successfully. Great leaders understand that change is an opportunity for growth and innovation and foster a culture that embraces and thrives in periods of change.

KEY TAKEAWAY

---

4. Leadership in the Community

Being involved in the community is an key aspect of great leadership. Effective leaders recognize that their influence and impact extend beyond organizational boundaries and into the broader community. By actively engaging with the community, understanding its needs, and collaborating with stakeholders, leaders can contribute to positive social change and make a lasting difference.

To engage with the community, leaders must first take the time to understand its needs and challenges. They listen to community members, engage in conversations, and conduct thorough research to gain insights into the issues that matter most. By understanding the unique characteristics and dynamics of the community, leaders can develop informed strategies and initiatives that address its specific needs.

Building relationships is a key component of community engagement. Effective leaders connect with community members, stakeholders, and organizations, fostering trust, collaboration, and mutual understanding. They actively participate in community events, meetings, and initiatives, demonstrating their commitment to the well-being of the community. By establishing strong relationships, leaders create a network of support and collaboration, leveraging collective resources and expertise to drive positive change.

In addition to building relationships, leaders collaborate with stakeholders to address community challenges. They seek partnerships with local organizations, government agencies, nonprofits, and other community leaders to create a collective impact. Through collaboration, leaders leverage diverse perspectives, resources, and expertise, fostering innovative solutions and maximizing the potential for positive change. By facilitating collaboration, leaders empower the community to take ownership of its challenges and work together towards shared goals.

Effective leaders also act as advocates for the community, amplifying its voice and raising awareness of key issues. They use their influence and platform to advocate for policies, programs, and initiatives that benefit the community. By speaking out on behalf of the community, leaders bring attention to important matters and create opportunities for positive change at a broader level.

Leaders engage community members in decision-making processes, ensuring that their voices are heard and their perspectives are considered. They create opportunities for community input and feedback, inviting diverse opinions and ideas. By involving community members in the decision-making process, leaders empower them to take an active role in shaping their own future and contribute to the development of solutions that best meet their needs.

Engaging with the community is a continuous process. Effective leaders remain committed to long-term engagement, understanding that sustained efforts are necessary to drive lasting change. They establish mechanisms for ongoing dialogue and collaboration, ensuring that community engagement is embedded into the fabric of their leadership approach.

Engaging with the community is an integral aspect of effective leadership. By actively listening, building relationships, collaborating with stakeholders, advocating for the community, and involving community members in decision-making, leaders contribute to positive social change. Effective leaders understand that their influence extends beyond organizational boundaries and have a profound impact on the communities they serve.

KEY TAKEAWAY

Initiating Positive Change

Initiating positive change is a core aspect of community leadership. Effective leaders recognize the social, economic, and environmental challenges facing their communities and take action to address them. By volunteering their time, advocating for change, and leveraging available resources, leaders make a tangible difference and inspire others to join their efforts.

Volunteering is a powerful way for leaders to contribute to positive change within their communities. By actively engaging in volunteer activities, leaders demonstrate their commitment to addressing local challenges. They donate their time, skills, and expertise to support community organizations, initiatives, and projects. Volunteering allows leaders to directly impact the lives of community members, whether through serving meals at a local shelter, tutoring students, or participating in environmental clean-up activities.

Advocacy is another crucial aspect of community leadership. Effective leaders use their platform and influence to advocate for the needs and concerns of their community. They raise awareness about important issues, educate others, and engage in conversations with key stakeholders, including government officials, policymakers, and community organizations. Through their advocacy efforts, leaders aim to bring about policy changes, secure resources, and promote sustainable solutions that address the underlying causes of community challenges.

In addition to volunteering and advocacy, leaders leverage available resources to drive positive change. They identify and mobilize resources, whether financial, human, or material, to support community initiatives. Leaders collaborate with businesses, nonprofits, and government agencies to secure funding, sponsorships, and partnerships that enhance the impact of their efforts. By leveraging resources effectively, leaders maximize their ability to create lasting change within their communities.

Effective leaders take a proactive approach to address community issues. They analyze local needs and identify gaps or opportunities for improvement. Leaders develop action plans and strategies that are grounded in research, data, and community input. They engage community members, seeking their perspectives and involvement in the decision-making process. By taking a proactive stance, leaders create a sense of urgency and inspire collective action to address community challenges.

Leaders inspire others to join their efforts and create a ripple effect of positive change. By modeling their commitment, passion, and dedication, leaders motivate community members to get involved and make a difference. They create platforms for community engagement, encourage collaboration, and foster a sense of ownership and empowerment among community members. Through their leadership, they build a network of like-minded individuals who share their vision for a better future.

KEY TAKEAWAY

Community leadership involves taking action to initiate positive change. Through volunteering, advocacy, and resource mobilization, leaders make a tangible difference in their communities. They take a proactive approach to address social, economic, and environmental challenges and inspire others to join their efforts. Community leaders have a profound impact on the well-being of their communities, creating a sense of hope, empowerment, and unity for all.

Inspiring and Empowering Others

One of the most important aspects of community leadership is motivating and empowering people. Effective leaders understand that their impact goes beyond their individual contributions and that true change can be achieved by inspiring and empowering others to become leaders in their own right. By serving as role models, offering support, and encouraging active citizenship, leaders cultivate a community of engaged individuals committed to positive transformation.

Leaders serve as role models by embodying the values and behaviors they wish to see in others. They lead by example, demonstrating integrity, compassion, and a commitment to service. By consistently demonstrating these qualities in their actions and decisions, leaders inspire others to follow suit and strive for excellence in their own lives.

Supporting others is a fundamental part of empowering individuals within the community. Leaders recognize the unique strengths and potential of those around them and provide the necessary resources, guidance, and mentorship to help them thrive. They offer encouragement, constructive feedback, and opportunities for growth and development. By investing in the growth and well-being of others, leaders inspire confidence and empower individuals to take on leadership roles and make a positive difference.

Leaders also encourage active citizenship within the community. They promote civic engagement, encouraging individuals to participate in community activities, initiatives, and decision-making processes. They educate community members about their rights, responsibilities, and the importance of being informed and involved. By fostering a sense of civic duty, leaders empower individuals to take an active role in shaping their community and driving positive change.

In addition to their direct influence, leaders create platforms and spaces for others to express their ideas, concerns, and aspirations. They facilitate dialogue, encourage diverse perspectives, and create opportunities for collaboration. By providing a forum for community members to contribute their voices and expertise, leaders foster a sense of ownership and collective responsibility for the community's well-being.

Effective leaders also celebrate the achievements and contributions of others. They recognize the efforts and successes of individuals within the community, acknowledging their impact and inspiring others to follow their lead. By shining a spotlight on the accomplishments of others, leaders create a culture of appreciation and encourage others to step up and make a difference.

KEY TAKEAWAY

Inspiring and empowering others is an essential aspect of community leadership. Leaders serve as role models, offer support, and encourage active citizenship. By investing in the growth and well-being of individuals within the community, leaders inspire confidence and empower others to take on leadership roles. Through their actions and initiatives, leaders cultivate a community of engaged individuals committed to positive transformation.

Summary

Leadership is not confined to formal titles or positions but is a mindset and a set of qualities that can be cultivated by anyone. By cultivating self-awareness, taking initiative, embracing personal growth, and demonstrating leadership within organizations and communities, individuals can make a significant impact and inspire positive change. Leadership is not an exclusive domain; it is accessible to all who are willing to step forward, lead with integrity, and motivate others to reach their full potential. You possess the capacity to lead and create a meaningful difference in your immediate surroundings. So, embrace your leadership potential, ignite your passion, and inspire others to join you on the journey of making the world a better place. Great leadership begins with you, right where you are.

Leadership
KEY CNCEPTS

Calm Confidence
Leaders Know and They Know That They Know

Introduction

Various skills and traits are included in the complicated and diverse idea of leadership. One of the key traits found in effective leaders is calm confidence. Calm confidence refers to a state of assurance and self-assurance where leaders possess a deep understanding of themselves, the situation at hand, and the knowledge that comes with it. They exhibit a sense of composure, trust in their abilities, and radiate a quiet but powerful confidence. We will explore the significance of calm confidence in leadership, discussing its characteristics, benefits, and how it contributes to the success of leaders and their teams.

1. Characteristics of Calm Confidence

Leaders who exhibit calm confidence demonstrate these key characteristics:

Self-Awareness

Self-awareness is the first aspect of calm confidence in leadership. Effective leaders who possess calm confidence have a deep understanding of themselves, including their strengths, weaknesses, values, and beliefs. They have taken the time to reflect on their own identity and have a clear understanding of what they bring to the table as leaders.

Self-awareness allows leaders to recognize their own limitations and areas for growth. They understand that no one is perfect and that seeking advice or input from others can lead to better decisions and outcomes. They are not afraid to ask for help or delegate tasks to others who may be better suited for certain responsibilities. By acknowledging their own limitations, calm confident leaders create an environment of trust and openness, where team members feel comfortable offering their expertise and insights.

Furthermore, self-awareness enables leaders to make sound judgments and decisions. By understanding their own values and beliefs, they can align their actions and decisions with their core principles. They have a clear sense of their own goals and priorities, allowing them to make choices that are consistent with their personal and professional values. This alignment brings a sense of authenticity and integrity to their leadership approach.

Self-aware leaders are also open to feedback and criticism. They actively seek out opportunities for growth and development and are willing to accept feedback from their team members, superiors, and peers. They understand that feedback is a valuable tool for self-improvement and that it can lead to personal and professional growth. By embracing feedback, calm confident leaders demonstrate humility and a commitment to continuous learning.

Moreover, self-awareness enables leaders to manage their emotions and maintain composure in challenging situations. They have a clear understanding of their emotional triggers and can regulate their emotions effectively. This ability to remain calm and composed inspires confidence in their team members and allows for rational decision-making, even in high-pressure situations.

KEY TAKEAWAY

Self-awareness is a critical component of calm confidence in leadership. Leaders who possess self-awareness have a clear understanding of their strengths, weaknesses, values, and beliefs. They are aware of their own limitations and actively seek feedback from others. By aligning their actions with their core principles and managing their emotions effectively, self-aware leaders inspire trust, make sound judgments, and create an environment that encourages openness and growth. Self-awareness is a continuous process that allows leaders to evolve, adapt, and lead with calm confidence.

Emotional Stability

Emotional stability is the second key trait of effective leaders. Leaders who maintain emotional stability exhibit composure, confidence, and control, even in the face of challenging situations. This stability enables them to navigate through adversity, make sound decisions, and inspire confidence in their teams.

When leaders remain calm and composed, they create a sense of stability and assurance within their teams. In times of uncertainty or crisis, their ability to control their emotions provides a steady anchor for others to rely on. This stability helps to alleviate fear, anxiety, and panic, enabling team members to focus on problem-solving and maintaining productivity.

One of the key benefits of emotional stability in leaders is the ability to think and respond rationally. By keeping their emotions in check, leaders can objectively assess situations, analyze information, and make well-informed decisions. They are less likely to be swayed by impulsive reactions or succumb to the pressures of the moment. Instead, they maintain a clear and rational mindset, which allows them to identify potential solutions and navigate through complex challenges.

Emotionally stable leaders also possess the ability to remain empathetic and understanding towards their team members. While they control their emotions, they are attuned to the emotions and needs of others. This empathy allows them to connect with their team on a deeper level, providing support and guidance when needed. By being emotionally stable, leaders create an environment where open communication and trust can thrive.

Leaders who maintain emotional stability serve as role models for their teams. Their calm and confident demeanor inspire confidence and trust in their abilities. Team members feel reassured knowing that their leader can handle difficult situations with composure. This trust cultivates a sense of loyalty and respect, encouraging team members to give their best and follow the leader's example.

To maintain emotional stability, leaders often develop self-awareness and practice self-regulation. They understand their own triggers and tendencies and work to manage their emotional responses accordingly. This may involve techniques such as deep breathing, mindfulness, or seeking support from mentors or coaches. By proactively managing their emotions, leaders can more effectively maintain stability in challenging situations.

Resilience

Resilience is the third key attribute of leaders who possess calm confidence. These leaders understand that setbacks and failures are inevitable in any endeavor, and they approach challenges with a mindset focused on growth and learning. Rather than being discouraged by setbacks, they view them as opportunities for improvement and development.

Leaders with calm confidence demonstrate a strong belief in their abilities and have an unwavering determination to overcome obstacles. They maintain a positive attitude and remain optimistic even in the face of adversity. Their resilience allows them to bounce back from setbacks quickly and continue moving forward.

In times of failure or setback, calm confident leaders assess the situation objectively. They analyze what went wrong, identify the lessons to be learned, and use that knowledge to adjust their approach. They are not afraid to take responsibility for mistakes or failures and see them as valuable experiences for personal and professional growth.

Leaders with resilience inspire their teams to persevere. They understand that challenges can be demotivating and create a sense of uncertainty. However, by exhibiting resilience, leaders show their teams that setbacks are temporary and can be overcome. They provide support and encouragement, reminding their team members of their collective capabilities and instilling confidence in their ability to navigate through difficulties.

Calm confident leaders also foster a culture of resilience within their teams. They encourage an open and transparent environment where team members feel comfortable discussing challenges and failures. By normalizing setbacks as part of the learning process, leaders create an atmosphere where team members are willing to take risks and innovate without fear of reprisal.

Leaders with resilience are flexible and adaptable. They understand that circumstances can change rapidly, and they are prepared to adjust their strategies and plans accordingly. They embrace change as an opportunity for growth and adaptation. Their ability to remain composed and flexible in the face of uncertainty enables them to lead their teams effectively through transitions and navigate new challenges with ease.

Resilience is a critical attribute of leaders who possess calm confidence. These leaders view setbacks and failures as learning opportunities and exhibit unwavering determination to find solutions. They inspire their teams to persevere and create a culture of resilience within their organizations. By embracing challenges with a growth mindset and remaining flexible in the face of uncertainty, leaders with resilience not only overcome obstacles but also inspire their teams to achieve their full potential.

KEY TAKEAWAY

Decisiveness

Decisiveness is the fourth key trait exhibited by calm confident leaders. These leaders possess the ability to make timely and effective decisions with clarity and conviction. They understand the importance of gathering relevant information, analyzing it objectively, and drawing upon their knowledge and experience to inform their choices.

Calm confident leaders demonstrate a proactive approach to decision-making. They are not afraid to take calculated risks and make choices in the face of uncertainty. They understand that indecisiveness can lead to inefficiency and stagnation, and they actively seek to provide direction and clarity to their teams.

To make informed decisions, calm confident leaders gather information from various sources. They seek input from subject matter experts, consult data and analytics, and engage in dialogue with team members and stakeholders. By considering multiple perspectives, they are able to weigh the pros and cons of different options and make well-rounded decisions.

However, calm confident leaders also understand the importance of timely decision-making. They recognize that prolonged analysis and deliberation can lead to missed opportunities or delays in progress. They set clear deadlines for decision-making and maintain a sense of urgency without sacrificing the thoroughness of their decision-making process.

Drawing upon their knowledge and experience, calm confident leaders bring a wealth of insights to their decision-making. They rely on their expertise and understanding of the situation to make sound judgments. Their confidence in their abilities allows them to trust their instincts and make decisions based on a combination of data, experience, and intuition.

Decisiveness instills trust and confidence in team members. When leaders make decisions with clarity and conviction, it provides a sense of direction and stability to the team. Team members feel assured that their leader has carefully considered all relevant factors and has made a decision that is in the best interest of the team and the organization. This trust creates a cohesive and focused team environment where individuals can work together towards common goals.

Decisive leaders promote accountability and action within their teams. They set clear expectations and provide clear guidelines for implementation. By making decisions confidently, leaders create a culture of accountability, where team members are empowered to take ownership of their tasks and responsibilities.

KEY TAKEAWAY

Decisiveness is a critical characteristic of calm confident leaders. These leaders possess the ability to make decisions with clarity and conviction. They gather information, analyze it objectively, and draw upon their knowledge and experience to make informed choices. Their decisiveness instills trust, provides direction, and promotes accountability within their teams. By being decisive, calm confident leaders inspire their teams to take action and move forward towards achieving their goals.

2. Benefits of Calm Confidence in Leadership

Leaders who exhibit calm confidence experience numerous benefits, both personally and within their teams. These benefits include trust and respect, stability and reassurance, effective decision making, team engagement and motivation, and adaptability and agility.

Trust and Respect

Trust and respect are key elements of effective leadership, and calm confident leaders have a unique ability to inspire both within their teams. Their unwavering self-assurance and composed demeanor create an environment of trust, where team members feel secure in their leader's abilities and decisions.

Calm confident leaders build trust through consistency and reliability. They consistently demonstrate their competence, expertise, and commitment to their team's success. By delivering on their promises and consistently meeting expectations, they establish a track record of reliability, fostering trust among their team members. Their calm and composed demeanor in the face of challenges reassures team members that they are capable of handling difficult situations.

Transparency and open communication are also key factors in building trust. Calm confident leaders are honest and transparent in their interactions with their teams. They provide clear and timely information, share their thought processes behind decisions, and actively listen to the concerns and feedback of their team members. This transparency creates a sense of psychological safety, where team members feel comfortable expressing their opinions and ideas without fear of judgment or retribution.

In addition, calm confident leaders empower their team members by delegating authority and providing autonomy. They trust their team members' capabilities and give them the freedom to make decisions and take ownership of their work. By empowering their team members, leaders demonstrate their trust in their abilities and create a sense of respect and autonomy within the team.

Furthermore, calm confident leaders lead by example and treat others with respect and dignity. They value diversity and inclusivity, fostering an environment where all team members feel valued and respected. They actively listen to different perspectives, encourage collaboration, and create opportunities for growth and development. By treating others with respect, leaders earn the respect of their team members in return.

When team members trust and respect their leader, they are more likely to be engaged, motivated, and committed to achieving shared goals. They feel secure in their leader's abilities and decisions, allowing them to focus on their work without unnecessary concerns or doubts. Trust and respect create a positive and supportive team culture, enabling open communication, collaboration, and innovation.

Stability and Reassurance

Stability and reassurance are significant contributions of calm confident leaders. They understand the importance of providing a sense of stability and security to their teams, especially during times of uncertainty or change. Through their composed and measured approach, they instill confidence in their teams and alleviate anxieties that may arise in dynamic situations.

Calm confident leaders act as an anchor for their teams during turbulent times. They remain composed and maintain a steady demeanor, even when faced with challenges or unexpected changes. Their ability to stay calm under pressure reassures team members that there is a strong and stable presence guiding them through difficulties.

During times of uncertainty or change, calm confident leaders communicate effectively and transparently with their teams. They provide clear and consistent information, sharing the reasons behind decisions and offering reassurance about the future. By keeping their teams well-informed, leaders minimize uncertainty and create a sense of stability within the team.

Calm confident leaders proactively address concerns and anxieties that may arise in their teams. They are approachable and accessible, providing opportunities for open dialogue and actively listening to the concerns and perspectives of team members. By acknowledging and addressing these concerns, leaders demonstrate their commitment to supporting their teams and creating a secure environment.

Calm confident leaders also lead by example in maintaining a positive attitude and resilience during challenging times. They emphasize the importance of staying focused, adapting to change, and finding opportunities for growth and learning. Their unwavering optimism and confidence in the team's ability to navigate through difficulties instills a sense of reassurance and inspires team members to persevere.

In addition, calm confident leaders create a supportive environment where team members feel comfortable sharing their concerns and seeking guidance. They provide mentorship and guidance to help team members navigate through uncertainties or changes. By offering support and being available to provide guidance, leaders contribute to the stability and reassurance within the team.

The stability and reassurance provided by calm confident leaders enable team members to focus on their work and perform at their best. It alleviates anxieties, fosters a sense of security, and allows team members to channel their energy into productive efforts. When team members feel secure and reassured, they are more likely to take risks, be creative, and contribute to the team's success.

> *Calm confident leaders play a crucial role in providing stability and reassurance to their teams. Through their composed approach, effective communication, proactive addressing of concerns, and supportive environment, they instill confidence and alleviate anxieties during times of uncertainty or change. The stability and reassurance created by calm confident leaders enable teams to navigate through challenges, adapt to change, and thrive in dynamic environments.*

KEY
TAKEAWAY

Effective Decision Making

Effective decision-making is a key attribute of leaders with calm confidence. These leaders possess the ability to make well-informed decisions based on their knowledge and expertise. Their composed and focused demeanor allows them to analyze situations objectively, consider multiple perspectives, and ultimately make choices that lead to effective and efficient outcomes.

Calm confident leaders understand the importance of gathering relevant information before making decisions. They take the time to gather data, consult subject matter experts, and seek input from team members and stakeholders. By considering various perspectives and gathering diverse insights, they have a more comprehensive understanding of the situation at hand.

Analyzing situations objectively is a crucial aspect of effective decision-making. Leaders with calm confidence are able to detach themselves from personal biases or emotional attachments, enabling them to make rational and logical judgments. They assess the available information, evaluate potential risks and opportunities, and weigh the pros and cons of different options.

Considering multiple perspectives is another strength of leaders with calm confidence. They understand that diverse viewpoints can provide valuable insights and challenge their own assumptions. These leaders actively seek input from team members and stakeholders, encouraging open and constructive dialogue. By considering multiple perspectives, they make well-rounded decisions that take into account the needs and interests of various stakeholders.

Calm confident leaders also draw upon their knowledge and expertise when making decisions. They leverage their experience and understanding of similar situations to inform their choices. Their confidence in their own abilities and expertise allows them to trust their judgment and make decisions based on a combination of data, experience, and intuition.

When making decisions, leaders with calm confidence also take into account the potential impact on the team and the organization as a whole. They consider long-term implications and strategic alignment. Their decisions are not solely based on immediate benefits but also on the overall goals and vision of the team and organization.

Calm confident leaders recognize the importance of timeliness in decision-making. While they thoroughly analyze situations, they also understand the need for timely action. They set clear deadlines for decision-making and maintain a sense of urgency when necessary. Their ability to balance thoroughness and timeliness allows them to make effective decisions without unnecessary delays.

The ability to make effective decisions contributes to the success of leaders and their teams. By making well-informed choices, leaders provide clarity, direction, and guidance to their teams. Team members feel confident in their leader's ability to navigate complex situations and trust in the decisions made. Effective decision-making enables teams to work towards shared goals with a clear sense of purpose and direction.

Leaders with calm confidence demonstrate effective decision-making skills. They gather relevant information, analyze situations objectively, consider multiple perspectives, and draw upon their knowledge and expertise to make well-informed choices. Their ability to balance thoroughness and timeliness contributes to the success of their teams. By making effective decisions, leaders with calm confidence provide clarity, direction, and guidance, creating an environment where team members feel confident and motivated to achieve shared goals.

KEY TAKEAWAY

Team Engagement and Motivation

Team engagement and motivation are key outcomes of calm confident leaders. These leaders possess self-assurance and belief in their abilities, which radiates to their teams and inspires them to perform at their best. They create an environment where individuals feel empowered, motivated, and encouraged to contribute their best work.

Calm confident leaders lead by example. They demonstrate a strong belief in their own abilities and exhibit self-assurance in their actions and decisions. This self-assurance is contagious and inspires team members to believe in themselves and their own capabilities. By showcasing their confidence, leaders create a positive and motivating atmosphere where team members are encouraged to step out of their comfort zones and take calculated risks.

These leaders also encourage a growth mindset within their teams. They view challenges and setbacks as opportunities for learning and development. By embracing a culture of continuous improvement, they foster an environment where team members are motivated to enhance their skills, seek new knowledge, and pursue excellence in their work. The belief in ongoing growth inspires individuals to push beyond their limitations and strive for personal and professional growth.

Calm confident leaders empower their team members by providing autonomy and decision-making authority. They trust their team members' capabilities and create opportunities for them to take ownership of their work. By delegating responsibilities and providing a sense of autonomy, leaders encourage individuals to take initiative, make meaningful contributions, and feel a sense of ownership over their work. This empowerment boosts motivation and engagement within the team.

Calm confident leaders offer support and recognition to their team members. They provide guidance, mentorship, and coaching to help individuals develop their skills and overcome challenges. They acknowledge and appreciate the efforts and achievements of their team members, recognizing their contributions and providing feedback and recognition when warranted. This support and recognition foster a sense of belonging and motivation within the team.

Effective communication is another key aspect of team engagement and motivation. Calm confident leaders communicate openly and transparently, sharing information, goals, and expectations with their teams. They listen attentively to the ideas and concerns of their team members and provide clear and constructive feedback. By fostering a culture of open communication, leaders create a collaborative environment where team members feel valued and motivated to contribute their ideas and perspectives.

KEY TAKEAWAY

Calm confident leaders inspire and motivate their teams by embodying self-assurance, encouraging a growth mindset, empowering individuals, and providing support and recognition. Their belief in their own abilities and the capabilities of their team members creates an environment of empowerment and motivation. By fostering a culture of continuous growth, trust, open communication, and recognition, leaders with calm confidence inspire their teams to take risks, embrace challenges, and strive for excellence. This leads to increased engagement, productivity, and success within the team.

Adaptability and Agility

Adaptability and agility are key qualities of leaders with calm confidence. These leaders possess the ability to navigate through complex and rapidly changing environments with ease, adjusting their strategies and actions as needed. Their confidence allows them to embrace new ideas and perspectives, leading to innovative solutions and driving success in dynamic circumstances.

Leaders with calm confidence understand that change is inevitable and that the ability to adapt is crucial for continued success. They proactively monitor the external environment, staying abreast of industry trends, technological advancements, and shifts in the market. This awareness enables them to anticipate potential challenges and opportunities and adjust their approach accordingly.

In the face of change, leaders with calm confidence maintain a composed and focused demeanor. They do not succumb to panic or become overwhelmed by uncertainty. Instead, they approach new situations with a positive and open mindset, viewing them as opportunities for growth and improvement. Their confidence allows them to inspire their teams to embrace change and adopt a similar adaptive mindset.

These leaders are not afraid to challenge the status quo and explore new ideas and perspectives. They actively seek input from their team members, encourage diverse thinking, and foster an environment where innovation thrives. By embracing new ideas and perspectives, they tap into the collective intelligence of their team and leverage the power of collaboration to find creative solutions to complex problems.

Leaders with calm confidence are quick to adjust their strategies and actions when necessary. They recognize the importance of flexibility and agility in a rapidly changing landscape. They are willing to deviate from established plans and make necessary course corrections to adapt to evolving circumstances. Their confidence allows them to make informed decisions swiftly, without hesitation or second-guessing.

By demonstrating adaptability and agility, leaders with calm confidence instill confidence in their teams. They create a sense of stability and reassurance, even in times of uncertainty. Team members feel supported and encouraged to embrace change, knowing that their leader is flexible and adaptable. This mindset promotes a culture of innovation and resilience, enabling the team to overcome challenges and capitalize on opportunities.

KEY TAKEAWAY

Adaptability and agility are vital qualities exhibited by leaders with calm confidence. These leaders embrace change, adjust their strategies, and adopt new perspectives to navigate through complex and rapidly changing environments. Their confidence allows them to inspire their teams to embrace change, challenge the status quo, and find innovative solutions. By fostering a culture of adaptability and agility, leaders with calm confidence create a resilient and innovative team that can thrive in any dynamic circumstance.

3. The Power of Knowledge and Self-Assurance

The power of knowledge and self-assurance is undeniable when it comes to calm confidence in leadership. Effective leaders recognize that their confidence is rooted in a deep understanding of themselves, the situation at hand, and the knowledge they possess. They actively seek opportunities for learning and growth to stay informed about industry trends, developments, and best practices. This commitment to continuous learning strengthens their confidence and equips them with the knowledge needed to make informed decisions, inspire their teams, and navigate challenges with ease.

Leaders who possess calm confidence understand that knowledge is dynamic and ever-evolving. They acknowledge that they don't have all the answers and actively seek feedback and different perspectives. By seeking diverse viewpoints, they gain a broader understanding of complex issues and challenges, which enhances their decision-making ability. They value the input of others and create an environment that encourages open dialogue, collaboration, and knowledge-sharing.

Continuous learning is a key aspect of their self-assurance. These leaders understand that personal and professional growth requires a commitment to ongoing development. They invest time and effort in expanding their knowledge and skills, whether through formal education, training programs, mentorship, or self-directed learning. By continuously seeking new knowledge, they stay ahead of the curve and remain relevant in a rapidly changing world.

The self-assurance of calm confident leaders comes from a deep-rooted belief in their own abilities and the knowledge they have acquired over time. They have developed a strong sense of self-awareness and a clear understanding of their strengths, weaknesses, values, and passions. This self-assurance enables them to lead authentically and with conviction, knowing that they have the knowledge and expertise to navigate challenges effectively.

Calm confident leaders understand the importance of surrounding themselves with a diverse and talented team. They recognize that they don't need to have all the answers and value the expertise of those around them. They create an environment that fosters collaboration and encourages team members to contribute their knowledge and insights. By leveraging the collective intelligence of their team, they strengthen their own knowledge base and enhance their decision-making capabilities.

The power of knowledge and self-assurance in leadership extends beyond the individual leader. It permeates the entire organization or team, creating a culture of continuous learning and growth. When leaders demonstrate a commitment to knowledge acquisition and self-assurance, they inspire and motivate their team members to do the same. This shared pursuit of knowledge fosters a sense of collective confidence and empowers individuals to contribute their best work.

> *The power of knowledge and self-assurance is integral to calm confidence in leadership. Effective leaders understand that their confidence is rooted in a deep understanding of themselves, the situation, and the knowledge they possess. They continuously seek opportunities for learning and growth, value diverse perspectives, and surround themselves with a talented team. This commitment to knowledge strengthens their confidence, enhances their decision-making abilities, and inspires their teams to achieve greatness.*

KEY TAKEAWAY

Summary

Calm confidence is a powerful characteristic of effective leaders. It stems from a deep understanding of oneself, the situation at hand, and the knowledge that comes with it. Leaders with calm confidence possess self-awareness, emotional stability, resilience, decisiveness, and adaptability. The benefits of calm confidence include trust, stability, effective decision-making, team engagement, and adaptability. Leaders who exhibit calm confidence inspire their teams, create a sense of security, and navigate through challenges with ease. They understand that their confidence is rooted in continuous learning, knowledge acquisition, and self-assurance. In a world where uncertainty is prevalent, calm confidence empowers leaders to navigate complexity, inspire others, and achieve success in their leadership endeavors.

Leadership
KEY C🔓NCEPTS

3

Be at Your Best Regardless
How You Do Anything Is How You Do Everything

Introduction

Leadership is not limited to specific situations or roles; it is a way of life. Great leaders understand that their actions and behaviors in all aspects of life reflect their true character and commitment to excellence. The old adage "How you do anything is how you do everything" encapsulates the idea that leaders strive to bring their best selves to every situation, regardless of its significance. We will explore the concept of being at your best regardless and how it applies to leadership in various contexts.

1. Consistency and Integrity

Consistency and integrity are fundamental principles that guide leaders who embrace the philosophy of being at their best regardless. These leaders recognize the importance of aligning their actions with their values and principles, regardless of the circumstances they face.

Consistency is key in demonstrating leadership. Leaders who are consistent in their actions earn the trust and respect of their team members and stakeholders. They understand that their behavior sets the tone for the entire organization and that inconsistency can lead to confusion and erode trust. By consistently demonstrating their values and principles, leaders create a sense of stability and reliability within their teams.

Leaders who prioritize consistency understand that their actions speak louder than words. They do not waver in their commitment to excellence, integrity, and ethical behavior. They understand that their consistent actions send a powerful message to their team members, stakeholders, and the broader community.

Integrity is another essential element for leaders who embrace this philosophy. Leaders with integrity adhere to a strong moral and ethical compass. They act in alignment with their values and principles, even when faced with difficult choices or temptations. Their decisions are guided by a sense of honesty, fairness, and transparency.

Leaders with integrity inspire trust and confidence in their teams. Team members feel secure knowing that their leader acts with integrity, and they can rely on their leader's judgment and decision-making. This trust creates a strong foundation for collaboration and teamwork, enabling the team to work cohesively towards shared goals.

In addition, leaders with integrity foster an environment of ethical behavior within their organizations. They set clear expectations and hold themselves and others accountable for their actions. They promote a culture of honesty, transparency, and accountability, where unethical behavior is not tolerated.

Consistency and integrity go hand in hand. Consistency reinforces integrity, and integrity strengthens consistency. Leaders who consistently demonstrate integrity build a reputation of trustworthiness and authenticity. They are seen as individuals who stand by their principles, even in challenging times.

Leaders who prioritize consistency and integrity lead by example. They understand that their actions speak louder than words and that their behavior has a direct impact on the behavior of others. By consistently demonstrating integrity, they inspire their team members to do the same. This cascading effect fosters a culture of integrity and ethical behavior throughout the organization.

KEY TAKEAWAY

Leaders who embrace the philosophy of being at their best regardless prioritize consistency and integrity. They understand that their actions must align with their values and principles, regardless of the circumstances they face. Consistency builds trust and reliability, while integrity fosters ethical behavior and inspires others.

2. Excellence and Attention to Detail

Excellence and attention to detail are core values for leaders who embody the mindset of being at their best regardless. These leaders understand that achieving excellence requires a commitment to giving their best effort and paying attention to even the smallest details.

Leaders who prioritize excellence set high standards for themselves and their teams. They continuously strive for improvement, constantly seeking ways to enhance their skills and knowledge. They do not settle for mediocrity but consistently aim to exceed expectations. By demonstrating a commitment to excellence, these leaders inspire and motivate their teams to reach for greatness.

Attention to detail is a critical aspect of achieving excellence. Leaders who pay attention to the details understand that success is often found in the small things. They recognize that even minor oversights or errors can have significant consequences. By being meticulous and thorough in their approach, they ensure that every aspect of their work is of the highest quality.

Leaders who prioritize attention to detail inspire trust and confidence. Their meticulousness in planning, organizing, and executing tasks instills a sense of reliability and precision. Team members feel assured that their leader has carefully considered all aspects of a project, reducing the risk of mistakes and enhancing the overall outcome.

Leaders who pay attention to detail foster a culture of excellence within their teams. They encourage team members to take pride in their work and to strive for perfection. By setting a high standard for attention to detail, these leaders cultivate a sense of ownership and accountability among their team members, leading to improved performance and outcomes.

Attention to detail also enhances problem-solving and decision-making. Leaders who carefully analyze information and consider all relevant factors are better equipped to make informed decisions. By paying attention to the details, they can identify potential issues, mitigate risks, and seize opportunities. This level of thoroughness strengthens their ability to navigate complex challenges and achieve successful outcomes.

In addition, leaders who prioritize excellence and attention to detail create a positive and professional image for themselves and their organizations. Their commitment to quality and meticulousness in their work builds a reputation of reliability, competence, and professionalism. This reputation attracts talented individuals and fosters positive relationships with stakeholders.

KEY TAKEAWAY

Leaders who embrace the mindset of being at their best regardless prioritize excellence and attention to detail. They set high standards for themselves and their teams, continuously striving for improvement and excellence in all aspects of their work. Their meticulousness and commitment to quality inspire trust and confidence, foster a culture of excellence, and enhance problem-solving and decision-making. By embodying these values, leaders create a positive image for themselves and their organizations, driving success and making a lasting impact.

3. Resilience and Perseverance

Resilience and perseverance are essential qualities for leaders who embrace the philosophy of being at their best regardless. These leaders understand that setbacks and challenges are an inherent part of the leadership journey. They approach difficult situations with a growth mindset, viewing obstacles as opportunities for growth and learning.

Resilient leaders maintain a positive attitude and remain focused on their goals, even in the face of adversity. They bounce back from setbacks and setbacks with determination and an unwavering belief in their abilities. Instead of being discouraged by obstacles, they see them as stepping stones on the path to success. Their resilience inspires and motivates their team members to persevere and overcome challenges as well.

Moreover, resilient leaders understand that setbacks and failures are valuable learning experiences. They analyze these experiences, seeking to understand the root causes and identifying areas for improvement. They use setbacks as opportunities for personal and professional growth, developing new strategies and skills to overcome similar challenges in the future. By embracing a growth mindset, these leaders foster a culture of continuous improvement and resilience within their teams.

Perseverance is another key characteristic of leaders who embrace the philosophy of being at their best regardless. They do not give up easily, even when faced with significant obstacles or prolonged difficulties. They are willing to put in the necessary time, effort, and dedication to achieve their goals. They understand that success often requires persistence and a willingness to push through challenges.

Leaders who persevere inspire their team members to do the same. They demonstrate tenacity and determination, showing that setbacks are temporary roadblocks rather than insurmountable barriers. Their perseverance creates a sense of belief and confidence within their teams, encouraging individuals to stay committed to their goals and overcome obstacles along the way.

In addition, resilient and persevering leaders recognize the importance of self-care and maintaining their well-being. They understand that to be at their best regardless, they need to prioritize their physical and mental health. They practice self-care strategies such as exercise, rest, and mindfulness to recharge and replenish their energy. By taking care of themselves, they are better equipped to handle challenges and setbacks with resilience and perseverance.

Resilient and persevering leaders create an environment that supports and nurtures their team members' resilience. They encourage open communication, provide support and resources, and celebrate individual and team achievements. By fostering a culture of resilience, they empower their team members to bounce back from setbacks, learn from failures, and embrace challenges as opportunities for growth.

Resilience and perseverance are crucial qualities for leaders who embrace the philosophy of being at their best regardless. These leaders maintain a positive attitude, learn from setbacks, and use challenges as opportunities for growth. Their resilience and perseverance inspire and motivate their teams to overcome obstacles and strive for success. By embodying these qualities, leaders create a culture of resilience and empower their team members to navigate challenges with determination and resilience.

KEY
TAKEAWAY

4. Self-Discipline and Personal Growth

Self-discipline and personal growth are key aspects of leaders who embody the philosophy of being at their best regardless. These leaders recognize that self-discipline is the foundation for achieving excellence and that personal growth is essential for their ongoing development as leaders.

Self-discipline is the ability to control one's impulses, thoughts, and actions. Leaders who prioritize self-discipline understand that it is crucial for maintaining focus, overcoming distractions, and staying committed to their goals. They establish routines and habits that support their productivity and well-being. They manage their time effectively, setting priorities and avoiding procrastination. By practicing self-discipline, these leaders ensure that their actions align with their intentions and enable them to make consistent progress towards their objectives.

Personal growth is a lifelong journey for leaders who strive to be at their best regardless. These leaders embrace a growth mindset, understanding that they have the capacity to learn, improve, and develop new skills throughout their lives. They actively seek opportunities for learning and development, whether through formal education, training programs, conferences, or self-directed learning. They engage in continuous learning, staying abreast of industry trends, best practices, and emerging technologies.

Leaders committed to personal growth also seek feedback from others. They value different perspectives and welcome constructive criticism as a means for self-improvement. They actively seek opportunities to receive feedback, whether from their team members, mentors, or trusted colleagues. By embracing feedback, these leaders gain valuable insights into their strengths and areas for growth, enabling them to make necessary adjustments and continuously develop their leadership capabilities.

Leaders who prioritize personal growth actively seek out challenges and new experiences. They step outside of their comfort zones, taking on projects that stretch their abilities and expose them to new perspectives. They embrace ambiguity and uncertainty, recognizing that these situations provide fertile ground for personal and professional growth. By embracing challenges, they develop resilience, adaptability, and problem-solving skills.

Personal growth also involves reflection and self-awareness. Leaders who commit to being at their best regardless take time for introspection and self-reflection. They assess their strengths, weaknesses, values, and aspirations. They evaluate their progress, celebrate their achievements, and identify areas for improvement. By developing self-awareness, these leaders gain deeper insights into their leadership style, allowing them to lead with authenticity and make intentional decisions.

> *Self-discipline and personal growth are crucial components for leaders who strive to be at their best regardless. These leaders exhibit self-discipline in their habits, time management, and decision-making, enabling them to maintain focus and drive towards their goals. They actively pursue personal growth through continuous learning, seeking feedback, embracing challenges, and cultivating self-awareness. By prioritizing self-discipline and personal growth, leaders create a solid foundation for their ongoing development and maximize their potential as effective and impactful leaders.*

KEY TAKEAWAY

5. Relationships and Collaboration

Relationships and collaboration are foundational elements for leaders who embrace the philosophy of being at their best regardless. These leaders recognize that success is not achieved in isolation but through the collective efforts of a cohesive and engaged team. They prioritize building meaningful relationships and fostering a collaborative environment to drive positive outcomes.

Leaders who prioritize relationships understand the value of treating others with respect, empathy, and kindness. They actively listen to their team members, valuing their perspectives and ideas. By demonstrating genuine care and concern for the well-being and success of others, these leaders create an environment of trust and psychological safety. Team members feel comfortable sharing their thoughts, taking risks, and contributing their best work.

Leaders who prioritize relationships go beyond simply establishing connections. They invest time and effort in building authentic and meaningful relationships with their team members. They take an interest in their personal and professional development, offering guidance and support. These leaders understand that strong relationships are built on mutual trust, respect, and a genuine desire to see others succeed.

Effective collaboration is another key aspect for leaders who embrace the philosophy of being at their best regardless. These leaders understand that collaboration brings together diverse perspectives, skills, and strengths to achieve shared goals. They create an environment that encourages teamwork, open communication, and the sharing of ideas. By fostering a collaborative culture, they unlock the collective potential of their team and promote innovation and creativity.

Leaders who prioritize relationships and collaboration actively seek input and feedback from their team members. They value diverse perspectives and understand that the best solutions often emerge from collective efforts. These leaders encourage open dialogue, create opportunities for brainstorming, and promote a culture of inclusive decision-making. By involving their team members in the decision-making process, they not only enhance the quality of decisions but also foster a sense of ownership and commitment among team members.

In addition, leaders who prioritize relationships and collaboration understand the power of recognition and appreciation. They celebrate the achievements and contributions of their team members, acknowledging their efforts and successes. This recognition fosters a positive and supportive environment where team members feel valued and motivated to continue giving their best effort.

Leaders who prioritize relationships and collaboration extend their focus beyond their immediate team. They foster relationships and collaboration with stakeholders, partners, and other leaders in their industry or community. They recognize that strong external relationships can lead to new opportunities, partnerships, and collective impact.

KEY TAKEAWAY

Leaders who embody the philosophy of being at their best regardless prioritize relationships and collaboration. They create a supportive and inclusive environment where team members feel valued, empowered, and motivated to contribute their best work. By building meaningful relationships, fostering collaboration, and valuing diverse perspectives, these leaders unlock the collective potential of their teams and drive positive outcomes.

6. Impact and Legacy

Impact and legacy are paramount for leaders who embrace the principle of being at their best regardless. These leaders recognize that their actions and decisions hold the power to shape the future and leave a lasting impression on those they lead and the organizations they serve.

Leaders committed to making a positive impact understand that their choices extend beyond their personal gain or immediate results. They consider the broader implications of their decisions and strive to align them with their values, ethics, and long-term goals. They prioritize the greater good over short-term gains, ensuring that their actions have a positive impact on their team members, stakeholders, and the community at large.

These leaders inspire others through their commitment to excellence. By consistently giving their best effort and upholding high standards, they set a positive example for their team members. Their dedication to continuous improvement and learning motivates others to pursue excellence and strive for personal and professional growth. They foster a culture of achievement, where individuals are encouraged to push boundaries, innovate, and surpass expectations.

Integrity is a cornerstone of the impact and legacy that leaders strive to leave behind. Leaders who prioritize integrity make decisions and take actions guided by honesty, transparency, and ethical principles. They hold themselves accountable and expect the same from their team members. By demonstrating unwavering integrity, these leaders create an environment of trust and respect, where individuals feel safe and valued.

Leaders who focus on impact and legacy understand the importance of nurturing talent and developing future leaders. They actively invest in the growth and development of their team members, providing mentorship, guidance, and opportunities for advancement. They empower individuals to reach their full potential and make their own positive impact on the organization and society. By cultivating the next generation of leaders, they create a legacy that extends beyond their own tenure.

These leaders also embrace innovation and embrace change as a means of creating a lasting impact. They encourage creativity and open-mindedness, empowering their team members to think outside the box and challenge the status quo. They foster a culture of continuous improvement and adaptability, ensuring that their organizations remain relevant and resilient in a rapidly changing world.

In addition, leaders focused on impact and legacy understand the importance of collaboration and partnerships. They actively seek opportunities to collaborate with other organizations, stakeholders, and community members to address complex challenges and drive positive change. By leveraging collective intelligence and resources, they maximize their impact and leave a legacy of collaboration and collective impact.

KEY TAKEAWAY

Leaders who embrace the principle of being at their best regardless strive to make a positive impact and leave a lasting legacy. They prioritize the greater good, inspire through their commitment to excellence and integrity, and empower others to reach their full potential. By nurturing talent, embracing innovation, and fostering collaboration, these leaders create a positive and lasting imprint on their teams, organizations, and the communities they serve. Their impact extends far beyond their immediate sphere of influence, leaving a legacy of positive change and transformation.

Summary

Being at your best regardless is not just a slogan; it is a mindset and a way of life for effective leaders. Great leaders understand that how they do anything is how they do everything and strive to bring their best selves to every situation, big or small. By prioritizing consistency, integrity, excellence, resilience, self-discipline, relationships, and making a positive impact, leaders inspire others and leave a lasting legacy. Embracing this philosophy fosters personal and professional growth, enhances leadership effectiveness, and paves the way for a successful and fulfilling leadership journey.

The Certain Way
Leaders Do Things in a Certain Way

Introduction

The idea of leadership has many facets and encompasses more than just getting things done. It encompasses the way leaders approach their roles, the mindset they adopt, and the behaviors they exhibit. Great leaders understand that their actions and attitudes play a crucial role in determining their effectiveness and the outcomes they achieve. They recognize that there is a certain way to lead that encompasses specific principles, values, and practices. We will delves into the concept of "The Certain Way" in leadership and explore how it shapes successful leadership behaviors.

1. Values-Based Leadership

Values-based leadership is a cornerstone of "The Certain Way" in leadership. Leaders who prioritize values understand that their actions and decisions should align with their core principles. They establish a clear set of values that serve as a moral compass, guiding their behavior and decision-making processes. These leaders recognize that values-based leadership goes beyond achieving goals; it is about upholding integrity, ethics, and a sense of purpose.

By leading with values, leaders create an environment of trust and respect. When their actions consistently align with their stated values, they inspire confidence and build credibility among their team members and stakeholders. Employees feel secure knowing that their leader operates with a strong moral compass and is committed to doing what is right. This fosters a positive organizational culture where everyone understands the importance of ethical behavior and shares a common commitment to core values.

Leaders who prioritize values also act as role models for their teams. They demonstrate integrity, authenticity, and accountability in their actions, motivating others to do the same. When leaders uphold their values, it sets a standard for behavior that encourages team members to follow suit. This creates a culture of trust, where individuals feel safe to express their opinions, take risks, and contribute their best work.

Values-based leadership helps leaders navigate complex decisions and dilemmas. When faced with difficult choices, leaders can refer to their values as a guide, ensuring that their decisions align with their principles and are consistent with the organization's mission and vision. This approach helps leaders maintain a sense of ethical responsibility and enables them to make decisions that are not only effective but also aligned with the organization's long-term objectives and societal impact.

Values-based leadership also promotes a sense of authenticity. When leaders align their actions with their values, they exhibit transparency and honesty. They demonstrate that their values are not just empty rhetoric but deeply held beliefs that guide their leadership style. This authenticity fosters stronger relationships with team members, stakeholders, and customers, as it creates an atmosphere of trust and reliability.

KEY TAKEAWAY

Values-based leadership is an integral part of "The Certain Way" in leadership. Leaders who prioritize values ensure that their actions and decisions align with their core principles. They inspire trust and respect from their team members and stakeholders by leading with integrity and authenticity. Values-based leadership guides decision-making processes, sets a standard for behavior, and fosters a positive organizational culture. By embracing values as a guide, leaders create a sense of purpose and create a lasting impact on their teams and organizations.

2. Purpose-Driven Leadership

Purpose-driven leadership is a fundamental aspect of "The Certain Way" in leadership. Leaders who prioritize purpose understand the importance of having a clear understanding of why they are leading and the impact they aim to make. They go beyond simply pursuing goals; they have a deep sense of purpose that drives their actions and guides their decision-making.

Leaders who lead with purpose are able to articulate their vision and mission in a compelling and inspiring manner. They communicate their purpose effectively to their team members, stakeholders, and the broader organization. By sharing their vision, they create a sense of meaning and direction, fostering a collective understanding of the organization's purpose and goals.

When leaders lead with purpose, they create a shared vision that aligns individual efforts with the broader organizational mission. They inspire their teams to connect their work to a greater purpose, which increases motivation, engagement, and commitment. Team members understand that their contributions are part of a larger picture and have a meaningful impact on the organization and the world around them.

Purpose-driven leaders also create a sense of meaning and fulfillment among their team members. When individuals understand the purpose behind their work, they are more likely to feel a sense of fulfillment and satisfaction. They are driven by intrinsic motivation, knowing that their efforts contribute to something greater than themselves. This sense of purpose enhances productivity, creativity, and innovation within the team.

Purpose-driven leaders are resilient and adaptable in the face of challenges. They understand that obstacles are inevitable on the path to achieving their purpose, but they remain focused and determined. When leaders and team members are driven by a higher purpose, they are more likely to persevere through difficulties and setbacks, finding innovative solutions and adapting to changing circumstances.

Purpose-driven leadership also attracts and retains top talent. In today's competitive job market, employees are increasingly seeking meaningful work that aligns with their values and provides a sense of purpose. Leaders who lead with purpose are able to attract individuals who share their vision and are passionate about making a difference. Moreover, purpose-driven leaders create an environment where individuals can thrive and find personal fulfillment in their work.

KEY TAKEAWAY

Purpose-driven leadership is a crucial component of "The Certain Way" in leadership. Leaders who prioritize purpose have a clear understanding of why they are leading and the impact they aim to make. By effectively communicating their purpose, they inspire and align their teams, creating a sense of meaning and direction. Purpose-driven leaders foster intrinsic motivation, enhance resilience, attract top talent, and create a fulfilling work environment. By leading with purpose, leaders can achieve extraordinary results and make a lasting impact on their teams and organizations.

3. Emotional Intelligence

Emotional intelligence is a key aspect of leadership for those who embrace "The Certain Way." Leaders who prioritize emotional intelligence possess a deep understanding of their own emotions, as well as the ability to empathize and connect with the emotions of others. They leverage emotional intelligence to build strong relationships, communicate effectively, and navigate conflicts in a sensitive and graceful manner.

Self-awareness is a key component of emotional intelligence. Leaders who are self-aware have a clear understanding of their own emotions, strengths, weaknesses, and triggers. They are in tune with their feelings and recognize how their emotions impact their behavior and decision-making. This self-awareness allows them to regulate their emotions and respond to situations in a balanced and constructive manner.

In addition to self-awareness, leaders who prioritize emotional intelligence demonstrate empathy towards others. They are attuned to the emotions and needs of their team members, stakeholders, and colleagues. They listen actively and seek to understand the perspectives and experiences of others. By showing empathy, these leaders create a sense of psychological safety and foster an environment where individuals feel heard, valued, and supported.

Emotionally intelligent leaders excel in communication. They possess the ability to convey their thoughts and ideas effectively, taking into account the emotional context of the situation. They are skilled in active listening, seeking to understand before being understood. By communicating with empathy and sensitivity, these leaders foster open dialogue, build trust, and create a positive and inclusive culture.

Conflict resolution is another area where emotionally intelligent leaders excel. They approach conflicts with a calm and composed demeanor, seeking to find win-win solutions. They are skilled at managing emotions, both their own and those of others, during difficult conversations. By recognizing and validating the emotions of individuals involved in the conflict, these leaders create an environment where conflicts can be resolved with respect and understanding.

Emotionally intelligent leaders also inspire and motivate others. They understand the impact of their emotions and attitudes on team morale and motivation. They are adept at recognizing and acknowledging the achievements and efforts of their team members, providing meaningful feedback, and fostering a positive work environment. By leveraging emotional intelligence, these leaders cultivate a sense of trust, collaboration, and loyalty among their teams.

Emotionally intelligent leaders are skilled at managing stress and maintaining their own well-being. They understand the importance of self-care and stress management to sustain their own emotional resilience. By taking care of their own emotional needs, they are better equipped to support and guide others.

> *Emotional intelligence is a vital component of leadership for those who embrace "The Certain Way." Leaders who prioritize emotional intelligence possess self-awareness, empathy, effective communication skills, conflict resolution abilities, and the capacity to inspire and motivate others. By leveraging emotional intelligence, these leaders build strong relationships, communicate effectively, and navigate conflicts with sensitivity and grace. They create a positive and inclusive work environment, fostering trust, collaboration, and high levels of engagement among their teams.*

KEY TAKEAWAY

4. Authenticity and Transparency

Authenticity and transparency are vital qualities for leaders who embrace "The Certain Way." These leaders understand that being genuine and honest is crucial for building trust and credibility among their team members and stakeholders. They prioritize open communication, encourage transparency in their actions and decision-making, and create an environment where individuals feel comfortable expressing their thoughts and ideas.

Authentic leaders are true to themselves and their values. They lead with integrity, acting in alignment with their beliefs and principles. They do not hide behind a facade but instead present their true selves to others. By being authentic, leaders foster a sense of trust and credibility among their team members. When team members see their leaders consistently displaying authenticity, they feel secure in knowing that their leader's actions align with their words.

Transparency is another key aspect of leadership for those who follow "The Certain Way." Transparent leaders are open and honest in their communication. They share information openly, providing context and reasoning behind their decisions. They are upfront about challenges, opportunities, and potential risks. Transparent leaders believe that sharing information empowers their team members and fosters a culture of trust and accountability.

By embracing authenticity and transparency, leaders create a culture of openness and mutual respect. When leaders are authentic, team members feel more comfortable being themselves and expressing their ideas and concerns. This openness encourages collaboration, innovation, and creativity. It also promotes psychological safety, allowing team members to take risks and learn from their mistakes without fear of judgment or reprisal.

Authentic and transparent leaders also value feedback. They actively seek input from their team members and stakeholders, recognizing that diverse perspectives lead to better decision-making. They create channels for open and honest feedback, inviting others to share their thoughts, concerns, and ideas. By valuing and acting upon feedback, these leaders demonstrate their commitment to continuous improvement and organizational growth.

Authenticity and transparency contribute to a leader's credibility and influence. When leaders are genuine and transparent, team members are more likely to trust their intentions and follow their lead. Authentic leaders inspire loyalty and commitment, as their actions align with their words. By being open and honest, leaders create an environment where individuals feel valued and heard, fostering stronger relationships and collaboration.

> *Authenticity and transparency are critical for leaders who follow "The Certain Way." By being true to themselves and their values, leaders foster trust and credibility among their team members. By embracing transparency in their actions and decision-making, leaders create an environment of openness and mutual respect. Authentic and transparent leaders encourage collaboration, innovation, and psychological safety. They value feedback, inspire loyalty, and foster strong relationships. By embodying authenticity and transparency, leaders can create a positive and thriving organizational culture.*

KEY TAKEAWAY

5. Continuous Learning and Adaptability

Continuous learning and adaptability are essential for leaders who embrace "The Certain Way." These leaders understand that the world is constantly evolving, and to stay effective, they must continually expand their knowledge and skills. They prioritize personal and professional growth, actively seeking opportunities for learning and development.

Continuous learning involves a commitment to acquiring new knowledge, staying informed about industry trends, and understanding emerging technologies and best practices. Leaders who prioritize continuous learning seek out formal education, attend conferences and workshops, engage in self-study, and actively pursue new experiences and challenges. They understand that by continuously learning, they can broaden their perspectives, enhance their problem-solving abilities, and make more informed decisions.

Adaptability is closely linked to continuous learning. Leaders who prioritize adaptability understand that change is inevitable, and they must be flexible in their thinking and approach. They embrace new ideas, technologies, and ways of working, and encourage their teams to do the same. These leaders are open to feedback and different perspectives, recognizing that innovation often comes from exploring new possibilities and challenging the status quo.

By prioritizing continuous learning and adaptability, leaders inspire their teams to be open to change and innovation. They create a culture of curiosity and growth, where individuals feel encouraged to explore new ideas and approaches. This fosters creativity, agility, and resilience within the organization, allowing it to adapt and thrive in a rapidly changing world.

Leaders who prioritize continuous learning and adaptability also lead by example. They demonstrate a growth mindset and actively share their own learning journeys and experiences. This openness encourages their team members to embrace learning and personal development, fostering a culture of continuous improvement.

Leaders who prioritize continuous learning and adaptability are better equipped to navigate uncertainty and ambiguity. They are agile in their thinking and can quickly pivot their strategies and actions in response to changing circumstances. Their ability to adapt enables them to seize opportunities and effectively address challenges, ensuring the long-term success of the organization.

KEY TAKEAWAY

Continuous learning and adaptability are crucial for leaders who follow "The Certain Way." By prioritizing personal and professional growth, leaders stay ahead of the curve and enhance their decision-making abilities. Embracing adaptability allows leaders to navigate change effectively and inspire their teams to be open to new ideas and innovative approaches. Continuous learning and adaptability foster a culture of growth, innovation, and resilience, ensuring the organization's long-term success in a dynamic and evolving world.

6. Empowerment and Delegation

Empowerment and delegation are integral aspects of leadership for those who embrace "The Certain Way." Leaders who prioritize empowerment understand that by giving their team members the authority and responsibility to make decisions and contribute their unique talents, they create an environment where individuals can thrive and excel. These leaders trust their team members' capabilities and provide guidance and support when needed.

Empowerment is about creating a sense of ownership and accountability among team members. Leaders who empower their teams provide clear expectations, goals, and boundaries, but also give individuals the freedom to determine how to achieve those objectives. This autonomy allows team members to tap into their creativity and problem-solving skills, leading to increased engagement and motivation. By empowering their teams, leaders create a culture of ownership, where individuals take pride in their work and feel a sense of responsibility for the team's success.

Delegation is another crucial aspect of empowerment. Leaders who delegate effectively match tasks and responsibilities to individuals' strengths and expertise. They trust their team members to carry out their assigned tasks and provide support and guidance when needed. Delegation not only distributes the workload but also empowers team members to take on new challenges and develop their skills. It promotes growth and development within the team and builds a bench of capable future leaders.

Empowering leaders also provide support and mentorship to their team members. They offer guidance and feedback, helping individuals develop their skills and overcome obstacles. These leaders create a safe space for open communication, where team members feel comfortable seeking advice and sharing their ideas. By offering support, leaders enable their team members to grow, learn, and reach their full potential.

In addition to individual growth, empowerment and delegation foster a collaborative and innovative work environment. When team members are empowered, they feel valued and included in the decision-making process. They contribute their unique perspectives and ideas, leading to greater creativity and innovation. By fostering collaboration and encouraging diverse voices, leaders create a culture of trust and inclusivity.

Empowerment and delegation enhance the leader's ability to focus on strategic and high-level tasks. By entrusting their team members with responsibilities, leaders free up their time and mental bandwidth to focus on strategic planning, relationship-building, and driving the organization forward. This allows leaders to leverage their skills and expertise in areas where they can have the greatest impact.

Empowerment and delegation are essential for leaders who follow "The Certain Way." By empowering their teams, leaders create a sense of ownership, accountability, and engagement. Delegation enables individuals to develop their skills and contribute their unique talents. Empowering leaders provide support and guidance, foster collaboration and innovation, and create a culture of trust and inclusivity. By empowering their teams, leaders unleash the potential of their organizations and drive long-term success.

7. Servant Leadership

Servant leadership is another key aspect of leadership for those who embrace "The Certain Way." Leaders who prioritize servant leadership place the needs of their team members at the forefront and focus on serving and supporting them. They create a culture of collaboration and empowerment, fostering an environment where individuals can thrive and contribute their best work.

Servant leaders actively listen to their team members' concerns, ideas, and feedback. They create a safe and open space for communication, where everyone's voice is valued and respected. By listening attentively, these leaders gain a deeper understanding of their team members' needs, aspirations, and challenges. This understanding enables them to provide relevant guidance and support.

In addition to active listening, servant leaders provide guidance and mentorship to their team members. They understand that their role is not only to direct but also to facilitate growth and development. These leaders take the time to understand the individual strengths, talents, and aspirations of their team members and support their professional and personal growth accordingly. They provide opportunities for learning, offer constructive feedback, and act as mentors, empowering individuals to reach their full potential.

Servant leaders also foster a culture of collaboration. They create an inclusive environment where everyone's contributions are valued, and diversity of thought is encouraged. These leaders recognize that the collective intelligence and diverse perspectives of the team lead to better outcomes. By promoting collaboration, they encourage teamwork, innovation, and creativity.

Servant leaders lead by example. They model the behaviors and values they expect from their team members. They demonstrate empathy, integrity, and humility in their actions, creating a positive and ethical work culture. These leaders prioritize the well-being and development of their team members, understanding that their success is intrinsically tied to the success of the team.

Servant leadership also promotes a sense of empowerment among team members. When leaders prioritize the needs of their team members and actively support their growth, individuals feel valued and empowered. They are more likely to take ownership of their work, demonstrate initiative, and contribute their best efforts. Servant leaders create an environment where individuals feel inspired and motivated to excel.

Servant leadership is a central component of "The Certain Way" in leadership. Leaders who prioritize servant leadership focus on serving and supporting their team members. They actively listen, provide guidance and mentorship, foster collaboration, and create an empowering environment. By leading with a servant's heart, these leaders create a positive work culture and empower individuals to reach their full potential. Servant leadership drives team success and contributes to the overall success of the organization.

KEY TAKEAWAY

Summary

Leadership is more than just achieving results; it is about the way things are done. Leaders who embrace "The Certain Way" understand that their approach, mindset, and behaviors significantly influence their effectiveness and the outcomes they achieve. By embodying principles such as values-based leadership, purpose-driven leadership, emotional intelligence, authenticity and transparency, continuous learning and adaptability, empowerment and delegation, and servant leadership, leaders can shape successful leadership behaviors and make a positive impact on their teams and organizations. By following "The Certain Way," leaders can create a culture of excellence, collaboration, and growth, ultimately achieving long-term success and leaving a lasting legacy.

Leadership
KEY CONCEPTS

The Common Denominator of Success
Leaders Do What Failures Don't Like to Do

Introduction

Success is often the result of consistent effort, perseverance, and a willingness to do what others are unwilling to do. It is not just about talent or luck; it is about making choices and taking actions that propel individuals towards their goals. In the realm of leadership, the common denominator of success lies in the ability to do what failures don't like to do. Great leaders understand the importance of embracing challenges, overcoming obstacles, and making the necessary sacrifices to achieve their objectives. We will explore the concept of the common denominator of success in leadership and how leaders distinguish themselves by doing what others are unwilling to do.

1. Embracing Challenges and Taking Calculated Risks

Embracing challenges and taking calculated risks are essential qualities of successful leaders. Leaders who are willing to step outside of their comfort zones and tackle difficult tasks have a distinct advantage over those who shy away from challenges. They understand that growth and progress occur when they push themselves beyond their limits and embrace the unknown.

Leaders who embrace challenges recognize that each obstacle presents an opportunity for learning, growth, and innovation. They understand that the path to success is not always smooth and straightforward. Instead of being discouraged by challenges, they see them as stepping stones to greatness. These leaders approach challenges with a positive mindset, viewing them as valuable learning experiences that help them refine their skills and expand their knowledge.

Successful leaders are not afraid to take calculated risks. They understand that without risk, there can be no reward. They carefully assess the potential benefits and consequences of their actions, making informed decisions that have the potential to yield significant results. These leaders understand that playing it safe and staying within their comfort zones will not lead to extraordinary achievements. Instead, they embrace calculated risks, knowing that stepping outside of their comfort zones is necessary for personal and professional growth.

Embracing challenges and taking calculated risks require resilience, adaptability, and determination. When faced with obstacles or setbacks, successful leaders do not give up easily. They persevere and find alternative approaches to overcome challenges. They are adaptable, willing to adjust their strategies and plans as circumstances change. These leaders understand that the ability to adapt and pivot is crucial for long-term success.

By embracing challenges and taking calculated risks, leaders set an example for their teams. They inspire their team members to push beyond their limits, encouraging them to embrace new opportunities and tackle difficult tasks. They create a culture that fosters innovation, creativity, and continuous improvement. When leaders demonstrate their willingness to take risks and face challenges head-on, they create an environment where team members feel empowered to do the same.

KEY TAKEAWAY

Embracing challenges and taking calculated risks are fundamental qualities of successful leaders. Leaders who are willing to step outside of their comfort zones and tackle difficult tasks demonstrate resilience, adaptability, and determination. They understand that growth and progress occur when they push themselves beyond their limits. By taking calculated risks, they open themselves up to new opportunities and possibilities. These leaders inspire their teams and create a culture of innovation and continuous improvement. Embracing challenges and taking calculated risks are essential for personal and professional growth and are key factors in achieving success as a leader.

2. Persistence and Resilience in the Face of Failure

Persistence and resilience are essential qualities of successful leaders. While failure is often seen as a setback, successful leaders view it as a stepping stone to success. They understand that failure is a natural part of the journey and an opportunity for growth and improvement.

When faced with failure, successful leaders do not become discouraged or give up. Instead, they analyze their mistakes and learn from them. They take responsibility for their actions and make the necessary adjustments to improve their performance. These leaders understand that failure provides valuable insights and lessons that can contribute to future success.

Resilient leaders possess the ability to bounce back from failure and setbacks. They maintain a positive mindset and remain determined to achieve their goals. Instead of allowing failure to define them, they use it as fuel to propel themselves forward. Resilient leaders are not easily discouraged by obstacles and challenges. They maintain their focus, adapt their strategies, and persevere until they achieve their desired outcomes.

Moreover, successful leaders understand that failure is not the end of the road. They view it as a temporary setback that can lead to growth and improvement. They embrace a growth mindset, believing that their abilities can be developed through dedication and hard work. They see failure as an opportunity to learn, innovate, and refine their approach.

By persisting and remaining resilient in the face of failure, leaders inspire their teams to do the same. They create a culture that encourages learning from mistakes and promotes a healthy attitude towards failure. These leaders understand that failure is not a reflection of one's worth or potential, but rather an opportunity for growth and progress. They support and encourage their team members to take risks, learn from failures, and keep moving forward.

> *Persistence and resilience are critical qualities for successful leaders. They view failure as a stepping stone to success, learning from their mistakes and making necessary adjustments. Resilient leaders bounce back from setbacks and maintain a positive mindset, staying determined to achieve their goals. By embracing failure as an opportunity for growth and improvement, leaders inspire their teams and foster a culture of learning, resilience, and continuous improvement.*

KEY TAKEAWAY

3. Discipline and Consistency

Discipline and consistency are fundamental attributes of successful leaders. These leaders understand that achieving long-term success requires commitment and dedication. They establish routines and habits that align with their goals and objectives, and they demonstrate discipline in consistently following through with their actions.

Leaders who exhibit discipline prioritize their time and resources effectively. They understand the importance of setting clear priorities and allocating their energy towards activities that contribute to their overall vision. They avoid distractions and remain focused on the tasks that align with their goals. This discipline enables leaders to make progress consistently, even when faced with competing demands or challenges.

Consistency is also a key aspect of successful leadership. Leaders who are consistent in their actions and behaviors build trust and credibility among their team members. They set clear expectations and follow through on their commitments, which creates a sense of reliability and dependability. Consistent leaders are seen as reliable and predictable, which fosters a positive work environment and enhances the effectiveness of their leadership.

Discipline and consistency require self-control and a strong sense of purpose. Leaders who demonstrate discipline are able to resist the temptation of short-term gratification or instant rewards. They understand the importance of delayed gratification and are willing to put in the necessary time and effort to achieve long-term success.

Discipline and consistency are not only beneficial for leaders themselves but also for their teams. When leaders exhibit discipline and consistency, they set an example for their team members. They inspire their teams to adopt similar behaviors and work ethic, creating a culture of discipline and consistency. This culture promotes accountability, productivity, and a strong work ethic among team members.

Discipline and consistency also contribute to the development of good habits and routines. By consistently engaging in positive behaviors, leaders develop habits that support their goals and objectives. These habits become ingrained in their daily lives, making it easier to maintain discipline and consistency over time.

4. Making Sacrifices for the Greater Good

Making sacrifices for the greater good is a hallmark of successful leaders. These leaders understand that their role extends beyond personal gain and that their decisions and actions have a broader impact on the team, organization, or community they serve. They prioritize the collective goals and needs over their own individual interests.

Successful leaders are willing to work long hours and put in extra effort to ensure the success of the team or organization. They understand that achieving exceptional results often requires going above and beyond the minimum requirements. These leaders are willing to invest their time and energy to achieve the desired outcomes, even if it means sacrificing personal leisure or comfort.

Leaders also make tough decisions that may be necessary for the greater good, even if they are unpopular or challenging. They understand that effective leadership sometimes requires making difficult choices that may have short-term implications but lead to long-term benefits. These leaders possess the courage to make decisions that align with the organization's mission and values, even if they face resistance or criticism.

Stepping out of their comfort zones is another sacrifice leaders make for the greater good. They recognize that personal growth and organizational progress often require embracing new challenges and taking on unfamiliar roles. Successful leaders are willing to stretch themselves, learn new skills, and adapt to changing circumstances to drive success.

Leaders demonstrate selflessness and dedication in their commitment to the team or organization. They prioritize the needs of others and are willing to put their own interests aside. Whether it is supporting team members, mentoring others, or advocating for the organization's mission, these leaders show a genuine concern for the welfare and success of those they lead.

By making sacrifices for the greater good, leaders inspire others to do the same. They create a culture of commitment and excellence, where individuals are willing to go beyond their own self-interests and work collectively towards a shared vision. When team members see their leaders making sacrifices and exhibiting selflessness, they are more likely to follow suit and contribute their best efforts for the greater good.

KEY TAKEAWAY

Making sacrifices for the greater good is an essential characteristic of successful leaders. They prioritize the collective goals and needs over their own interests, willing to work long hours, make tough decisions, and step out of their comfort zones. Their selflessness and dedication create a culture of commitment and excellence, inspiring others to do the same. By making sacrifices for the greater good, leaders drive organizational success, create positive impact, and foster a sense of unity and purpose among those they lead.

5. Continuous Learning and Growth

Continuous learning and growth are fundamental to the success of leaders. Successful leaders understand that the world is constantly evolving, and staying relevant requires ongoing development and adaptation. They prioritize their personal and professional growth, recognizing that continuous learning is key to remaining effective and influential in their roles.

Leaders who prioritize continuous learning actively seek out opportunities to expand their knowledge and skills. They engage in formal education, attend workshops and conferences, participate in professional development programs, and pursue certifications. They understand that these activities provide valuable insights, expose them to new ideas, and enhance their expertise.

Result driven leaders cultivate a growth mindset. They believe that their abilities can be developed through effort, practice, and continuous learning. They embrace challenges and view setbacks as opportunities for growth and improvement. By adopting a growth mindset, leaders are more willing to take risks, explore new approaches, and innovate.

Continuous learning also enables leaders to stay ahead of industry trends and emerging technologies. They proactively seek out information and stay informed about the latest developments in their field. This knowledge allows them to make informed decisions and lead their teams effectively in an ever-changing environment. Leaders who are continuously learning are better equipped to anticipate challenges, identify opportunities, and adapt to new circumstances.

Continuous learning enhances a leader's ability to inspire and motivate their teams. When leaders are actively engaged in their own learning and growth, they set a positive example for their team members. They demonstrate a commitment to improvement and inspire their teams to do the same. By fostering a culture of continuous learning, leaders encourage their team members to develop their skills, expand their knowledge, and reach their full potential.

Continuous learning also fosters innovation and creativity within organizations. Leaders who are open to new ideas and perspectives create an environment that encourages creativity and problem-solving. They value diverse opinions and encourage their team members to challenge the status quo. By promoting continuous learning, leaders drive a culture of innovation, enabling their teams to generate fresh ideas and adapt to changing market demands.

KEY TAKEAWAY

Continuous learning and growth are essential components of successful leadership. Leaders who prioritize their own personal and professional development remain relevant, adaptable, and influential in their roles. They seek out opportunities for learning, cultivate a growth mindset, stay informed about industry trends, and inspire their teams to develop their skills and knowledge. By fostering a culture of continuous learning, leaders drive innovation, inspire their teams, and maintain a competitive edge in today's dynamic business environment.

Summary

In the realm of leadership, the common denominator of success lies in the willingness to do what failures don't like to do. Successful leaders embrace challenges, take calculated risks, persist in the face of failure, exhibit discipline and consistency, make sacrifices for the greater good, and prioritize continuous learning and growth. These qualities set leaders apart and propel them towards success. By doing what others are unwilling to do, leaders inspire their teams, drive organizational success, and create a lasting impact. Ultimately, the common denominator of success in leadership is the ability to make choices and take actions that lead to positive outcomes, even in the face of adversity.

Leadership
KEY CNCEPTS

Thoughts Become Things
Leaders Think in Pictures and Attract Things to Them

Introduction

Leadership is not only about taking action; it starts with the power of thought. The way leaders think influences their beliefs, decisions, and ultimately, the outcomes they attract. The idea that "thoughts become things" emphasizes the profound impact of thoughts on reality. Successful leaders understand that their thoughts shape their mindset, drive their actions, and attract opportunities and outcomes. We will explore the concept of leaders thinking in pictures and how this mindset can impact their leadership effectiveness.

1. Visualization: Creating a Mental Blueprint

Visualization is a powerful technique that allows leaders to create a mental blueprint of their desired outcomes. By using their imagination and engaging their senses, leaders can vividly picture what they want to achieve. This mental image serves as a guide, providing clarity and direction in their decision-making and actions.

When leaders visualize their goals, they are able to define them with precision and detail. They imagine not only the end result but also the journey and the steps required to get there. This clarity helps leaders establish a clear roadmap, identify potential obstacles, and determine the strategies and resources needed to achieve their objectives.

Visualization also helps leaders focus their energy and attention on their desired outcomes. By consistently visualizing success, leaders program their subconscious mind to seek opportunities and take actions aligned with their goals. This focused energy increases their motivation, determination, and commitment to achieving their vision.

Visualization activates the creative potential within leaders. By mentally experiencing their desired outcomes, leaders can tap into their creative abilities and generate innovative ideas and solutions. This creative thinking enables leaders to find new approaches, overcome challenges, and seize opportunities that align with their visions.

Visualization is not limited to personal goals; it can also be extended to the entire team or organization. Leaders can encourage their team members to visualize shared goals and objectives, fostering a collective sense of purpose and alignment. By aligning the mental images of team members, leaders create a powerful synergy that propels the entire group toward success.

To effectively engage in visualization, leaders can dedicate specific time and space for reflection and mental imagery. They can practice guided visualization exercises or create vision boards that visually represent their goals and aspirations. Regularly revisiting and reinforcing these mental images keeps leaders focused, motivated, and aligned with their desired outcomes.

It is important to note that visualization alone is not enough to achieve success. It must be accompanied by intentional action, perseverance, and a strategic plan. However, visualization serves as a powerful tool that empowers leaders to clarify their goals, focus their energy, stimulate creativity, and manifest their visions into reality.

KEY TAKEAWAY

Leaders who think in pictures understand the power of visualization as a tool for creating a mental blueprint of their desired outcomes. By vividly imagining their goals, they gain clarity, focus their energy, and activate their creative potential. Visualization serves as a guiding force that directs their decision-making and actions, leading them and their teams toward success. Through visualization, leaders unlock their full potential and set a clear direction for achieving their visions.

2. Positive Mindset: Harnessing the Power of Optimism

A positive mindset is a key characteristic of leaders who think in pictures. These leaders choose to adopt an optimistic perspective, focusing on possibilities, solutions, and opportunities rather than dwelling on limitations or setbacks. They understand the power of positivity in shaping their thoughts, emotions, and behaviors, and how it influences their leadership effectiveness.

Leaders with a positive mindset are resilient in the face of challenges. They view obstacles as temporary hurdles that can be overcome through creative problem-solving and perseverance. Instead of being discouraged by setbacks, they maintain an optimistic outlook and actively seek solutions. This resilience inspires their teams to remain motivated and persevere in the face of adversity.

Leaders with a positive mindset are highly motivated. They believe in their own abilities and have confidence in their team's potential. Their optimistic outlook fuels their drive to achieve their goals and encourages their teams to aim for excellence. Their enthusiasm is contagious and creates a positive and energizing work environment.

Leaders who think in pictures understand that their mindset affects their leadership style and the overall culture of their organization. They consciously choose to focus on positive aspects, encouraging their teams to adopt a similar mindset. By fostering a culture of optimism and possibility, they create an environment where individuals feel empowered, motivated, and inspired to contribute their best work.

A positive mindset also attracts positive energy. Leaders who radiate positivity tend to attract opportunities and like-minded individuals who share their optimistic outlook. This positive energy creates a virtuous cycle of success, where the leader's positive mindset influences the team's performance, leading to greater achievements and attracting even more positive outcomes.

In addition, leaders with a positive mindset create a culture of optimism and resilience within their teams. They celebrate successes, big or small, and provide support and encouragement during challenging times. This fosters a sense of trust, collaboration, and psychological safety, enabling team members to take risks, innovate, and grow.

To cultivate a positive mindset, leaders can practice gratitude and mindfulness. They can regularly acknowledge and appreciate the positive aspects of their work and express gratitude for the contributions of their team members. They can also engage in activities that promote self-care and well-being, such as exercise, meditation, or hobbies, to maintain a positive outlook and manage stress.

KEY TAKEAWAY

Leaders who think in pictures understand the power of a positive mindset in their leadership journey. By focusing on possibilities, solutions, and opportunities, they enhance their resilience, motivation, and ability to navigate challenges. Their positive energy inspires their teams and creates a culture of optimism and possibility. Through their optimistic outlook, leaders attract positive outcomes, foster collaboration, and create an environment conducive to success and growth.

3. Goal Orientation: Aligning Thoughts with Intention

Goal orientation is a fundamental characteristic of leaders who think in pictures. These leaders have a clear vision of their desired outcome and are committed to achieving it. They align their thoughts with their intentions and consistently remind themselves of their goals, maintaining a mental image of the desired outcome. This alignment allows them to stay focused, prioritize their efforts, and make decisions that are in line with their goals.

By aligning their thoughts with their intentions, leaders create a sense of purpose and direction. They have a deep understanding of what they want to achieve and why it is important. This clarity enables them to set specific, measurable, achievable, relevant, and time-bound (SMART) goals that serve as guiding principles for their actions.

Leaders who think in pictures consistently visualize their goals and the steps required to achieve them. They break down their goals into manageable tasks and create action plans that outline the necessary actions, resources, and timelines. This structured approach helps them stay focused on the most important priorities and make progress toward their goals.

Aligning thoughts with intentions enhances leaders' decision-making abilities. When faced with choices or opportunities, leaders who think in pictures evaluate them based on how well they align with their goals. They make decisions that are consistent with their vision, values, and long-term objectives.

This alignment ensures that their decisions are purposeful and contribute to their overall success.

Consistently aligning thoughts with intentions also fosters a sense of commitment and determination. Leaders who maintain a clear mental image of their desired outcome are more likely to persevere in the face of challenges and setbacks. They are driven by their vision and maintain a high level of motivation, even when obstacles arise.

To effectively align thoughts with intentions, leaders can engage in practices such as affirmations, goal setting, and visualization exercises. They can regularly review their goals, assess their progress, and make necessary adjustments. By consistently reinforcing their intentions through these practices, leaders ensure that their thoughts remain aligned with their goals and guide their actions.

> *Leaders who think in pictures align their thoughts with their intentions and goals. They maintain a clear mental image of their desired outcome and consistently remind themselves of their vision. This alignment enables them to stay focused, prioritize their efforts, and make decisions that are in line with their goals. By consistently aligning their thoughts with their intentions, leaders manifest their goals with greater clarity and intentionality, driving their success and achieving their desired outcomes.*

KEY
TAKEAWAY

4. Emotional Intelligence: Connecting Thoughts and Feeling

Emotional intelligence is a key aspect of leadership, and leaders who think in pictures recognize the profound connection between thoughts and emotions. They understand that thoughts generate feelings, which significantly influence their actions, behaviors, and overall leadership effectiveness. By managing their thoughts and emotions, these leaders create a positive and empowering environment that inspires their teams to perform at their best.

Leaders who think in pictures are aware of the thoughts that arise in their minds and consciously choose those that generate positive emotions. They understand that their thoughts shape their emotional state and, in turn, impact their behavior and interactions with others. By intentionally focusing on positive thoughts, such as confidence, enthusiasm, and gratitude, these leaders create a positive mindset that influences their actions and inspires others.

Leaders who think in pictures recognize the importance of emotional awareness and empathy. They understand their own emotions and can effectively identify and understand the emotions of others. This emotional intelligence allows them to connect with their team members on a deeper level, fostering trust, empathy, and positive relationships. By empathizing with the emotions of their team members, these leaders can respond in a supportive and compassionate manner, promoting a positive work environment.

Managing thoughts and emotions also enables leaders to respond rather than react to challenging situations. They are able to step back, assess the situation objectively, and choose their responses thoughtfully. By maintaining control over their emotional state, leaders who think in pictures can lead with clarity, composure, and empathy, even in high-pressure situations. This emotional intelligence fosters a culture of open communication, trust, and collaboration.

Leaders who think in pictures understand the impact of their own emotional state on the overall team dynamic. They recognize that their emotions can be contagious and have a ripple effect on their team members. By managing their own emotions and projecting a positive emotional state, these leaders create an environment where team members feel safe, motivated, and empowered to perform at their best.

To enhance emotional intelligence, leaders who think in pictures can engage in practices such as mindfulness, self-reflection, and emotional regulation exercises. These practices help them become more aware of their thoughts and emotions, develop empathy, and manage their emotional responses effectively.

KEY TAKEAWAY

Leaders who think in pictures understand the connection between thoughts and emotions. They consciously choose thoughts that generate positive emotions, manage their emotional state, and foster emotional intelligence. By managing their thoughts and emotions effectively, these leaders create a positive and empowering environment that inspires their teams to perform at their best. Emotional intelligence is a key aspect of leadership, and leaders who think in pictures harness its power to build strong relationships, promote collaboration, and drive success.

5. Attracting Opportunities: The Law of Attraction

The Law of Attraction is a concept that leaders who think in pictures embrace. They recognize that their thoughts and energy have the power to attract similar vibrations and opportunities into their lives. By maintaining a positive and focused mindset, these leaders harness the Law of Attraction to attract opportunities, resources, and people who align with their visions and goals.

Leaders who think in pictures understand that their thoughts and beliefs shape their reality. They actively cultivate positive thoughts, visualize their desired outcomes, and affirm their success. By consistently focusing on what they want to achieve, these leaders align their energy with their goals, attracting circumstances and opportunities that support their visions.

Leaders with a visual mindset recognize the importance of taking proactive steps to attract opportunities. They understand that it is not enough to simply visualize success; they must also take inspired action. By aligning their thoughts with intentional and purposeful action, these leaders create a powerful synergy that propels them toward their goals.

Leaders who think in pictures are also adept at recognizing and seizing opportunities when they arise. They have developed a keen sense of awareness and intuition that allows them to identify opportunities that align with their visions. They approach new possibilities with an open mind and a willingness to explore uncharted territories.

Additionally, leaders who think in pictures understand the power of collaboration and networking in attracting opportunities. They actively seek out connections with like-minded individuals and engage in meaningful relationships. By nurturing these relationships and collaborating with others, leaders expand their sphere of influence and create opportunities for growth, innovation, and success.

To effectively harness the Law of Attraction, leaders who think in pictures practice gratitude and maintain a positive mindset. They express gratitude for the opportunities they have and anticipate future successes with confidence. They surround themselves with positive influences, engage in self-care practices, and maintain a sense of balance in their personal and professional lives.

It is important to note that the Law of Attraction does not operate in isolation from hard work, dedication, and strategic planning. Leaders who think in pictures understand that they must actively pursue their goals, demonstrate competency, and create value. The Law of Attraction is a complementary tool that enhances their efforts and amplifies their results.

KEY TAKEAWAY

Leaders who think in pictures embrace the concept of the Law of Attraction. They understand that their thoughts and energy have the power to attract similar vibrations and opportunities. By maintaining a positive and focused mindset, taking inspired action, and cultivating meaningful relationships, these leaders attract circumstances, resources, and individuals that contribute to their success. The Law of Attraction is a powerful tool that, when combined with proactive effort and strategic planning, can elevate leaders and enable them to achieve their visions and goals.

6. Communication and Influence: Painting a Compelling Picture

Communication is a key aspect of leadership, and leaders who think in pictures understand the power of storytelling and visual imagery in conveying their vision and influencing others. They recognize that words alone may not be enough to effectively communicate complex ideas or inspire action. Instead, these leaders leverage the power of vivid language, metaphors, and visuals to paint a compelling picture that resonates with their audience.

By using storytelling techniques, leaders who think in pictures create narratives that captivate and engage their audience. They craft narratives that connect with people on an emotional level, appealing to their values, aspirations, and sense of purpose. These stories bring their vision to life, making it relatable and inspiring others to join their cause.

Metaphors are another powerful tool used by leaders who think in pictures. By using metaphorical language, they can simplify complex concepts and make them more accessible to others. Metaphors create a bridge between abstract ideas and concrete experiences, allowing people to better understand and connect with the leader's message. These metaphors resonate with people, making the leader's vision more tangible and relatable.

In addition to storytelling and metaphors, leaders who think in pictures use visual imagery to enhance their communication. They create visual representations of their vision through presentations, diagrams, or even physical objects. These visuals serve as a powerful tool for capturing attention, stimulating the imagination, and conveying complex ideas in a clear and memorable way.

By painting a compelling picture through their communication, leaders who think in pictures ignite passion and motivation within their teams. Their vivid language, metaphors, and visuals engage emotions and create a sense of shared purpose. This emotional connection inspires others to align their actions with the leader's vision and work towards its realization.

To effectively use storytelling and visual imagery in communication, leaders who think in pictures must understand their audience and tailor their messages accordingly. They adapt their communication style to resonate with different individuals, taking into account their backgrounds, values, and preferences. By connecting with their audience on a personal level, these leaders build trust, inspire loyalty, and foster a sense of belonging.

> *Leaders who think in pictures recognize the power of storytelling and visual imagery in communication. By using vivid language, metaphors, and visuals, they paint a compelling picture that engages emotions, ignites passion, and motivates their teams to action. Through their effective communication, these leaders inspire others to align their actions with their vision, creating a shared sense of purpose and driving success.*

KEY TAKEAWAY

Summary

"Thoughts become things: Leaders think in pictures and attract things to them." This statement encapsulates the profound influence of thought on leadership effectiveness. Leaders who think in pictures harness the power of visualization, positive mindset, goal orientation, emotional intelligence, and the Law of Attraction to create a reality aligned with their visions. By intentionally shaping their thoughts, leaders set the stage for success, attract opportunities, and inspire others to achieve greatness. When leaders think in pictures, they transform their aspirations into tangible outcomes and create a future that reflects their highest aspirations.

Leadership
KEY C⬤NCEPTS

Be Sold On Yourself
People Buy from Those They Know and Trust

Introduction

In the world of leadership and business, the concept of "be sold on yourself" emphasizes the importance of self-confidence and personal branding. It recognizes that people are more likely to engage and buy from leaders they know and trust. We will explore how leaders who are genuinely confident in themselves and establish strong relationships based on trust can effectively influence and inspire others, ultimately leading to success.

1. Building Self-Confidence

Building self-confidence is a critical aspect of leadership. Leaders who are sold on themselves understand the importance of cultivating a strong belief in their abilities and qualities. They recognize that self-confidence is contagious and can inspire confidence in others.

Leaders who are sold on themselves actively invest in personal growth and development. They seek opportunities to enhance their skills and knowledge, whether through formal education, training programs, or mentorship. By continuously expanding their expertise, leaders gain a sense of mastery and competence that boosts their confidence.

Taking risks is another characteristic of leaders who are sold on themselves. They understand that growth and success often come from stepping outside of their comfort zones and embracing new challenges. These leaders are not afraid to push boundaries, try new approaches, and learn from their failures. By embracing risks, they demonstrate their confidence in their abilities and their willingness to learn and adapt.

Leaders who are sold on themselves celebrate their successes, no matter how small or big. They recognize their achievements and acknowledge the progress they have made. By celebrating successes, leaders build a positive self-image and reinforce their belief in their capabilities. This positive mindset radiates to others and inspires confidence in their leadership.

Cultivating self-confidence requires self-awareness and a positive mindset. Leaders who are sold on themselves understand their strengths and leverage them to their advantage. They also recognize their weaknesses and actively work on improving them. This self-awareness allows them to present themselves authentically, confidently highlighting their strengths while acknowledging areas for growth.

Leaders who are sold on themselves project a positive image to those around them. They exhibit self-assured body language, speak with conviction, and convey a sense of optimism. Their confidence is not based on arrogance but rather on a genuine belief in their abilities and the value they bring to their team and organization.

When leaders are confident in themselves, they inspire trust and attract others to their cause. Their self-assurance creates a sense of stability and reassurance, instilling confidence in their team members and stakeholders. People are more likely to follow leaders who exude confidence and believe in their own capabilities.

KEY TAKEAWAY

Building self-confidence is crucial for leaders who are sold on themselves. By continuously investing in personal growth, taking risks, celebrating successes, and cultivating a positive mindset, leaders inspire confidence in others and attract followers to their cause. Self-confidence is a powerful attribute that enables leaders to navigate challenges, make tough decisions, and drive positive change.

2. Authenticity and Personal Branding

Authenticity and personal branding are integral components of being sold on oneself as a leader. Leaders who are authentic stay true to their values, beliefs, and principles, and they don't try to be someone they're not. They embrace their unique qualities, acknowledging their strengths and weaknesses with honesty and transparency. By being genuine, leaders establish trust and credibility with their team members, stakeholders, and followers.

Being authentic means expressing oneself sincerely and without pretense. Authentic leaders have a clear understanding of their values and purpose, and they align their actions and decisions accordingly. They do not compromise their principles for the sake of popularity or short-term gains. Instead, they maintain consistency between their words and actions, creating a sense of trust and reliability.

Personal branding is an intentional effort to shape one's reputation and identity. Leaders who are sold on themselves actively cultivate their personal brand, understanding that it communicates their unique value proposition to their audience. They define their brand by highlighting their strengths, expertise, and the specific value they bring to the table. By strategically managing their personal brand, leaders can differentiate themselves and make a memorable impression on others.

Personal branding involves understanding one's target audience and tailoring the message and image accordingly. Leaders who are sold on themselves consider how their personal brand aligns with the needs and expectations of their team members, stakeholders, and followers. They strive to communicate a consistent and compelling message that resonates with their audience, fostering a sense of connection and loyalty.

Authenticity and personal branding go hand in hand, as personal branding should be an authentic reflection of the leader's values, strengths, and unique qualities. Leaders who are sold on themselves understand that their personal brand is not about trying to be someone they are not, but rather about amplifying their genuine self and sharing their authentic story.

By being authentic and consciously cultivating their personal brand, leaders who are sold on themselves create a strong and trustworthy identity. They are perceived as consistent, reliable, and true to their values. This consistency builds confidence and credibility among their team members, stakeholders, and followers, making it easier for others to connect with their vision, ideas, and leadership.

KEY TAKEAWAY

Authenticity and personal branding are essential components of being sold on oneself as a leader. By staying true to their values, embracing their unique qualities, and intentionally shaping their personal brand, leaders establish trust, credibility, and a strong connection with their team members, stakeholders, and followers. When leaders are authentic and consistent in their personal brand, it becomes easier for others to buy into their vision and be inspired by their leadership.

3. Building Relationships and Trust

Building relationships and trust is a fundamental aspect of leadership. Successful leaders recognize that people are more likely to buy into their ideas, follow their guidance, and support their initiatives when there is a foundation of trust and a genuine connection.

Leaders who prioritize building relationships invest time and effort in getting to know their team members, stakeholders, and customers. They actively engage in conversations, listen attentively, and show genuine interest in understanding others' perspectives and needs. By taking the time to truly know and understand the individuals they work with, leaders demonstrate respect and create a sense of importance and value.

Open communication is another key component of building relationships and trust. Leaders who are effective communicators foster an environment where people feel comfortable sharing their thoughts, concerns, and ideas. They encourage open dialogue, actively seek feedback, and address issues or conflicts with empathy and respect. By fostering a culture of open communication, leaders establish trust and create a safe space for collaboration and innovation.

Empathy is a critical element in building relationships and trust. Leaders who demonstrate empathy show genuine care and understanding towards others. They put themselves in others' shoes, considering their perspectives and emotions. By showing empathy, leaders create a sense of connection, foster positive relationships, and build trust.

Consistency and reliability are essential in building trust. Leaders who consistently deliver on their promises and commitments build credibility and demonstrate their trustworthiness. They follow through on their actions and words, creating a reliable and predictable environment. By being consistent and reliable, leaders establish trust and confidence in their abilities.

Transparency is another crucial factor in building trust. Leaders who are transparent in their decision-making processes, communication, and actions create an environment of honesty and integrity. They are open about their intentions, share relevant information, and provide explanations for their decisions. By being transparent, leaders build trust and credibility, as people feel informed and included in the decision-making process.

> *Building relationships and trust requires time, effort, and authenticity. It involves genuinely caring about others, demonstrating empathy, engaging in open communication, and being consistent and transparent. Leaders who prioritize building relationships and trust create an environment where people feel valued, respected, and empowered. This foundation of trust enables leaders to influence, inspire, and lead effectively, as people are more willing to buy into their ideas and follow their guidance.*

KEY TAKEAWAY

4. Effective Communication

Effective communication is a hallmark of leaders who are sold on themselves. These leaders understand the power of communication in conveying their vision, inspiring others, and building trust. They excel in various aspects of communication, including listening, articulating their ideas, asking meaningful questions, and providing constructive feedback.

Leaders who are sold on themselves have a clear and compelling vision that they communicate with passion and conviction. They understand the importance of painting a vivid picture of the future and inspiring others to join them on the journey. Through their words, they convey their passion and enthusiasm, capturing the hearts and minds of their audience. They articulate their vision in a way that resonates with their audience, igniting excitement and commitment.

Listening is a critical component of effective communication. Leaders who are sold on themselves actively listen to their team members, stakeholders, and customers. They show genuine interest in others' perspectives and ideas, seeking to understand before being understood. By listening attentively, they foster trust and create a safe space for open dialogue and collaboration.

Leaders who are sold on themselves ask thoughtful questions. They understand that asking the right questions not only helps them gather information but also encourages critical thinking and active participation from others. By asking open-ended questions that promote reflection and exploration, they foster deeper understanding, generate new insights, and inspire creativity.

Providing meaningful feedback is another aspect of effective communication for leaders who are sold on themselves. They offer constructive feedback that is specific, timely, and focused on growth and development. They recognize the importance of feedback in helping individuals and teams improve and achieve their full potential. By providing feedback in a supportive and constructive manner, leaders build trust and inspire continuous improvement.

Transparency and openness are key elements of effective communication for leaders who are sold on themselves. They share information openly, communicate changes and decisions with clarity, and address concerns and questions honestly. This transparency creates an environment of trust and collaboration, where people feel informed and included in the decision-making process.

KEY TAKEAWAY

Leaders who are sold on themselves excel in effective communication. They have a clear and compelling vision that they communicate with passion and conviction. They actively listen, ask thoughtful questions, provide meaningful feedback, and promote transparency. By mastering effective communication, these leaders foster understanding, inspire commitment, and build strong relationships based on trust.

5. Delivering Value and Results:

Delivering value and results is a critical aspect of leadership. Leaders who are sold on themselves understand the importance of taking ownership of their responsibilities and driving outcomes. They set high standards for themselves and their teams, constantly striving for excellence and challenging the status quo.

These leaders encourage innovation and creativity, recognizing that new ideas and approaches can lead to breakthrough results. They foster a culture of continuous improvement, empowering their team members to think outside the box, take calculated risks, and bring forth innovative solutions. By encouraging and supporting innovation, leaders create an environment that fosters growth, learning, and adaptability.

Leaders who are sold on themselves empower their team members to achieve their full potential. They provide the necessary resources, guidance, and support for their team members to excel. They delegate authority and responsibility, allowing individuals to take ownership of their work and contribute their unique skills and perspectives. By empowering their teams, leaders create a sense of ownership, accountability, and motivation that drives results.

These leaders lead by example, demonstrating a strong work ethic, dedication, and a commitment to delivering value. They set clear expectations, communicate goals, and provide the necessary guidance and feedback to ensure alignment and progress. By modeling excellence, leaders inspire their team members to strive for their best and contribute to the collective success.

Delivering value and results reinforces trust and credibility among team members and stakeholders. When leaders consistently deliver on their promises and expectations, they establish a reputation for reliability and dependability. This trust becomes the foundation for effective collaboration, engagement, and shared success.

Leaders who are sold on themselves understand that delivering value and results is not solely about individual achievements but about driving collective success. They foster a collaborative and inclusive environment, promoting teamwork and synergy. They recognize and celebrate the contributions of their team members, acknowledging that it is through collective efforts that significant results are achieved.

> *Leaders who are sold on themselves understand the importance of delivering value and results. They set high standards, encourage innovation, empower their team members, and lead by example. By consistently delivering value, these leaders reinforce trust, credibility, and their commitment to excellence. Through their actions and achievements, they inspire their teams and stakeholders to strive for greatness and contribute to shared success.*

KEY TAKEAWAY

Summary

"Be sold on yourself: people buy from those they know and trust" emphasizes the importance of self-confidence, authenticity, trust-building, effective communication, and delivering value in leadership. Leaders who embody this concept inspire confidence and trust in others, fostering strong relationships and creating a foundation for success. By believing in themselves and establishing genuine connections, leaders become influential and compelling figures whom others are willing to follow. As a result, they are more likely to attract opportunities, inspire loyalty, and achieve their goals.

Leadership
KEY CNCEPTS

Words Don't Teach
Leaders Teach Through the Clarity of Their Own Example

Introduction

Leadership is not just about telling others what to do; it is about demonstrating through action. The concept of "Words Don't Teach: Leaders Teach Through the Clarity of Their Own Example" emphasizes the power of leading by example. Effective leaders understand that their actions carry more weight than their words alone. By embodying the values, behaviors, and principles they wish to instill in others, leaders have a profound impact on their teams and inspire them to reach their full potential. We will explore how leaders can effectively teach through their own actions and the impact it has on creating a culture of excellence.

1. Leading by Example

A crucial component of good leadership is setting an example for others. It involves aligning one's actions with their words and values, and consistently demonstrating the behaviors and qualities they expect from others. When leaders lead by example, they set the standard for their team members and establish a culture of accountability, integrity, and excellence.

One of the key benefits of leading by example is that it creates trust and credibility. When team members observe their leaders consistently practicing what they preach, it builds trust and confidence in their leadership. It shows that the leader is genuine, reliable, and committed to upholding the values and expectations they have set. This trust and credibility contribute to stronger relationships, increased engagement, and improved performance within the team.

Leading by example also fosters a sense of accountability among team members. When leaders consistently demonstrate the desired behaviors and hold themselves accountable for their actions, it sets an expectation for others to do the same. Team members are more likely to take ownership of their work, meet deadlines, and deliver results when they see their leader modeling a high level of accountability. This creates a culture of responsibility and helps drive individual and collective performance.

Setting a good example provides clarity and guidance for team members. When leaders consistently exhibit the behaviors and qualities they expect from others, it provides a clear roadmap for how to succeed. Team members can observe and learn from their leader's actions, enabling them to understand the expectations and standards in a tangible way. This helps align the team towards common goals and fosters a shared understanding of what it takes to be successful.

Leading by example also inspires and motivates team members. When leaders demonstrate passion, dedication, and a strong work ethic, it creates a positive and inspiring environment. Team members are more likely to be motivated and engaged when they see their leader's commitment and enthusiasm. Leading by example ignites a sense of purpose and inspires team members to go above and beyond in their work.

KEY TAKEAWAY

Leading by example is a powerful leadership approach that sets the standard for behavior and performance. It builds trust, fosters accountability, provides guidance, and inspires others to excel. Leaders who consistently demonstrate the behaviors and qualities they expect from others create a culture of accountability, integrity, and excellence. By leading by example, leaders can effectively influence and inspire their teams to achieve exceptional results.

2. Actions Speak Louder than Words

Actions speak louder than words. This age-old adage holds true in leadership as well. Leaders who teach through the clarity of their own example understand that their actions carry more impact than mere words. They recognize that their behaviors and actions set the tone for the organization and have a profound influence on their team members.

When leaders consistently demonstrate the behaviors they expect from others, it sends a powerful message. It shows that they are not just talking the talk, but also walking the walk. Their actions serve as a blueprint for others to follow, reinforcing the importance of those behaviors and creating a culture of accountability and integrity.

By leading through their own example, leaders establish credibility and earn the trust of their team members. When team members witness their leaders taking responsibility, acting with integrity, and upholding high ethical standards, it fosters a sense of trust and confidence. Team members feel secure in following their leaders because they know they can rely on them to do what they say they will do.

Actions also have a greater impact in terms of inspiring and motivating others. Leaders who lead by example inspire their team members through their actions. When team members see their leaders putting in the effort, going the extra mile, and demonstrating a strong work ethic, it motivates them to do the same. Actions have a contagious effect, igniting a sense of commitment and dedication among the team.

A Leader's actions have a profound influence on the culture of the organization. When leaders exemplify the desired behaviors and values, it sets the standard for the entire organization. Team members take cues from their leaders and emulate their actions. This creates a culture where integrity, accountability, and excellence are valued and celebrated.

However, it is important to note that leaders are not infallible. They are human beings who may make mistakes. What sets effective leaders apart is their ability to acknowledge their mistakes, learn from them, and take corrective action. This level of humility and self-awareness further strengthens their credibility and reinforces the importance of owning up to one's actions.

3. Authenticity and Integrity

Authenticity and integrity are foundational principles for leaders who teach through their own example. These leaders understand the importance of aligning their actions with their values and principles, ensuring that there is consistency between what they say and what they do.

Authenticity is about being true to oneself and expressing one's genuine thoughts, emotions, and beliefs. Leaders who prioritize authenticity understand that their team members value transparency and honesty. They are comfortable being vulnerable and showing their true selves, which fosters trust and creates an environment where others feel safe to do the same. By being authentic, leaders build genuine connections with their team members and inspire them to bring their authentic selves to the workplace.

Integrity is about acting in alignment with one's values and moral principles. Leaders who lead with integrity consistently demonstrate ethical behavior and uphold high standards. They are accountable for their actions and take responsibility for their decisions. These leaders make ethical choices even in challenging situations, knowing that their actions have a ripple effect on their team members and the organization as a whole. By prioritizing integrity, leaders build trust and credibility, creating a culture of accountability and ethical conduct.

When leaders prioritize authenticity and integrity, they create an environment where people feel valued, respected, and inspired. Team members can trust that their leaders will act consistently with their values and principles. This consistency builds confidence and allows team members to align themselves with the shared vision and goals of the organization.

Leaders who prioritize authenticity and integrity inspire others to do the same. By setting an example of living according to one's values, leaders encourage their team members to identify and embrace their own values and act in alignment with them. This fosters a sense of purpose and fulfillment among team members and contributes to a positive and empowering work culture.

> *Leaders who teach through the clarity of their own example understand the importance of authenticity and integrity. By aligning their actions with their values and principles, these leaders build trust, credibility, and a positive work environment. They inspire their team members to bring their authentic selves to the workplace and act in alignment with their own values. Through authenticity and integrity, leaders create a culture where people feel safe, respected, and inspired to do their best work.*

KEY TAKEAWAY

4. Inspiring Excellence

Inspiring excellence is a hallmark of leaders who teach through the clarity of their own example. These leaders understand that their actions speak louder than words and that by embodying excellence themselves, they can inspire their teams to reach new heights of performance and achievement.

Leaders who inspire excellence set high standards for themselves and demonstrate a strong work ethic. They consistently deliver high-quality work and pay attention to the details, showing their team members what it means to strive for excellence in every task and project. These leaders lead by example, demonstrating a commitment to continuous improvement and a willingness to go above and beyond what is expected.

By modeling excellence in their decision-making, leaders demonstrate the importance of critical thinking, thorough analysis, and strategic foresight. They make informed decisions based on facts and data, considering the potential impact on the organization and its stakeholders. Their ability to make sound judgments inspires confidence in their team members and encourages them to approach decision-making with the same level of rigor and excellence.

Leaders who inspire excellence also foster a culture of continuous learning and growth. They encourage their team members to develop new skills, pursue professional development opportunities, and take ownership of their own learning. These leaders provide resources and support to facilitate growth, and they lead by example by engaging in their own continuous learning journeys. By valuing and promoting personal and professional growth, leaders create an environment where excellence is not just expected but actively cultivated.

Leaders who inspire excellence recognize and celebrate the achievements of their team members. They provide regular feedback and recognition, acknowledging the contributions and efforts of individuals and teams. This recognition serves as a motivator and reinforcement, inspiring team members to continue striving for excellence and delivering their best work.

KEY TAKEAWAY

Leaders who teach through the clarity of their own example inspire excellence in their teams. By embodying excellence in their work, decision-making, and attention to detail, these leaders set a high standard and motivate their team members to reach their full potential. Through their commitment to continuous learning, growth, and recognition, these leaders foster a culture of excellence where individuals are inspired to go above and beyond. By inspiring excellence, leaders drive organizational success and create a positive and high-performing work environment.

5. Creating a Learning Culture

Creating a learning culture is a key aspect of leaders who teach through their own example. These leaders understand the importance of continuous learning and development, not only for themselves but also for their teams. They recognize that a learning culture promotes innovation, adaptability, and resilience, which are essential for individual and organizational success.

Leaders who foster a learning culture prioritize their own learning and growth. They actively seek out new knowledge, skills, and perspectives, and they share their learning experiences with their teams. By demonstrating a commitment to their own development, these leaders set an example and inspire others to do the same.

These leaders provide resources and opportunities for learning and development. They encourage their team members to attend training programs, workshops, and conferences, and they provide access to relevant books, articles, and online resources.

By investing in the growth of their team members, leaders demonstrate their commitment to their success and create an environment where learning is valued and supported.

Leaders who foster a learning culture encourage curiosity and the exploration of new ideas. They create space for open dialogue, encourage questions, and promote a culture of continuous improvement. These leaders value diverse perspectives and encourage their team members to share their knowledge and insights. By creating an inclusive and collaborative environment, leaders enable their teams to learn from each other and collectively grow.

Importantly, leaders who foster a learning culture celebrate and recognize the achievements and efforts of their team members. They provide feedback, acknowledging the progress made and the skills developed. By recognizing and rewarding learning and growth, leaders reinforce the importance of continuous improvement and create a positive feedback loop that encourages further learning and development.

> *Leaders who teach through their own example foster a learning culture within their teams. By prioritizing their own learning, providing resources and opportunities for development, encouraging curiosity and open dialogue, and recognizing achievements, these leaders create an environment where learning is valued, supported, and celebrated. A learning culture promotes innovation, adaptability, and resilience, positioning the team and the organization for long-term success.*

KEY TAKEAWAY

6. Accountability and Ownership

Accountability and ownership are crucial aspects of leadership, and leaders who teach through their own example understand the importance of these qualities. They recognize that accountability and ownership foster a sense of responsibility and drive individual and team performance.

Leaders who promote accountability lead by example. They demonstrate a strong sense of personal accountability by taking ownership of their decisions, actions, and outcomes. They don't shy away from admitting mistakes or accepting responsibility when things go wrong. By showing vulnerability and accountability, these leaders create a culture where team members feel empowered to do the same.

These leaders set clear expectations and hold themselves accountable to the same standards they set for their team members. They communicate these expectations openly and ensure that everyone understands their role and responsibilities. By modeling accountability, leaders establish a norm where team members understand that their actions have consequences and that they are responsible for their performance and results.

Leaders who promote ownership encourage their team members to take ownership of their work and contribute their best effort. They empower their team members to make decisions and take initiative within their roles, fostering a sense of ownership and autonomy. These leaders provide support, resources, and guidance to enable their team members to succeed. By empowering their team members to take ownership, leaders create an environment where individuals feel a sense of pride and ownership in their work, leading to increased engagement and motivation.

Leaders who promote accountability and ownership provide feedback and recognition to reinforce these behaviors. They acknowledge and appreciate the efforts and achievements of their team members, creating a positive feedback loop that encourages continued accountability and ownership. By recognizing and celebrating individual and team successes, leaders create a culture where accountability and ownership are valued and celebrated.

KEY TAKEAWAY

Leaders who teach through their own example promote accountability and ownership. By demonstrating personal accountability, setting clear expectations, empowering their team members to take ownership, and providing feedback and recognition, these leaders create a culture of accountability and ownership. This culture drives individual and team performance, fosters a sense of responsibility, and ultimately contributes to the success of the organization.

7. Influence and Impact

Leaders who teach through their own example understand the power of influence and the far-reaching impact they have on their teams and organizations. They recognize that their actions, more than their words, carry weight and influence the behaviors and attitudes of their team members.

By consistently modeling the desired behaviors and values, leaders create a powerful ripple effect within their organization. When team members observe their leaders embodying integrity, collaboration, respect, and dedication, they are inspired to emulate those qualities. Leaders who lead by example set the standard for excellence and create a culture where those values are not just expected but embraced.

Through their actions, leaders demonstrate the importance of accountability, open communication, and continuous learning. They create an environment where team members feel comfortable and empowered to take risks, share their ideas, and contribute their best work. By modeling these behaviors, leaders foster a sense of trust and psychological safety, enabling their teams to thrive and unleash their full potential.

Leaders who lead by example also have a positive impact on the overall work environment. Their commitment to professionalism, positivity, and resilience sets the tone for the organization. Team members feel motivated, inspired, and supported by leaders who consistently demonstrate a strong work ethic and a positive attitude. This positive work environment promotes collaboration, innovation, and engagement, leading to increased productivity and overall success.

Leaders who teach through their own example influence not only their immediate team but also other leaders within the organization. Their actions inspire and motivate others to embrace similar leadership qualities and behaviors, creating a domino effect throughout the organization. By serving as role models, these leaders contribute to the development of a strong leadership pipeline, ensuring the continuity of a positive and influential leadership culture.

Leaders who teach through their own example have a significant influence and impact on their teams and organizations. Their actions and behaviors shape the culture, values, and performance of the organization. By consistently modeling the desired qualities, they inspire their teams to adopt those behaviors, creating a positive work environment and driving overall success. Through their influence, these leaders leave a lasting legacy and inspire future generations of leaders to lead with integrity, authenticity, and purpose.

KEY TAKEAWAY

Summary

The concept of "Words Don't Teach: Leaders Teach Through the Clarity of Their Own Example" highlights the importance of leading by example in effective leadership. Leaders who teach through their own example create a culture of accountability, excellence, and continuous learning. Their actions inspire and influence others, shaping behaviors and fostering a positive work environment. By consistently embodying the values and qualities they wish to instill in others, leaders have a profound impact on their teams and create a lasting legacy of leadership.

Leadership
KEY C◉NCEPTS

Sloppy Thinking
You Can't Create Past Your Own Beliefs

Introduction

In the realm of leadership, one of the critical factors that often determines success or failure is the quality of thinking. The concept of "sloppy thinking" highlights the importance of examining and challenging our own beliefs and assumptions to create meaningful and impactful outcomes. We will explore the notion that leaders cannot create beyond the limitations of their own beliefs and the significance of cultivating a mindset of critical thinking and intellectual curiosity.

1. The Influence of Beliefs

Leadership is heavily influenced by our beliefs. Our beliefs shape how we perceive ourselves, others, and the world around us. They influence our decision-making, our ability to take risks, and our willingness to embrace change. If leaders hold limiting beliefs or have a fixed mindset, it can have a significant impact on their effectiveness and the outcomes they can achieve.

Limiting beliefs are thoughts or beliefs that constrain our potential and hinder our ability to see possibilities and opportunities. These beliefs often stem from past experiences, societal conditioning, or self-imposed limitations. For example, a leader who believes that they are not capable of leading a successful project may hold themselves back from taking on challenging assignments or exploring innovative solutions. These beliefs create self-doubt and limit the leader's ability to inspire and motivate their team members.

Similarly, leaders with a fixed mindset believe that their skills, intelligence, or abilities are fixed traits and cannot be developed or improved. This mindset can hinder their willingness to learn, adapt, and embrace new ideas. It can create resistance to change and prevent leaders from exploring alternative perspectives or seeking feedback from their team members. As a result, the leader's growth and the growth of their team and organization may be stunted.

On the other hand, leaders who hold empowering beliefs and have a growth mindset believe in their own potential for growth and the potential of their team members. They embrace challenges, see failures as opportunities for learning, and actively seek out new knowledge and skills. These leaders are more open to taking calculated risks, experimenting with new approaches, and driving innovation within their teams and organizations. Their empowering beliefs inspire confidence, motivation, and a sense of possibility among their team members.

To overcome limiting beliefs and foster a growth mindset, leaders must engage in self-reflection and challenge their existing beliefs. This requires a willingness to question assumptions, seek feedback, and actively seek out opportunities for personal and professional growth. Leaders can benefit from self-development practices such as journaling, seeking mentors or coaches, and engaging in continuous learning. By actively working on their beliefs and mindset, leaders can expand their potential and create an environment that promotes growth and innovation.

KEY TAKEAWAY

The beliefs that leaders hold significantly influence their effectiveness and the outcomes they can achieve. Leaders with limiting beliefs or a fixed mindset unintentionally hinder their own growth and limit the potential for innovation and progress within their teams and organizations. Conversely, leaders with empowering beliefs and a growth mindset inspire confidence, foster growth, and drive innovation. By actively challenging and reshaping their beliefs, leaders can create a more positive and impactful leadership style that inspires their team members to reach new heights of success.

2. The Impact of Sloppy Thinking

Leaders who engage in sloppy thinking risk making decisions based on outdated or biased information, overlooking opportunities, and failing to adapt to changing circumstances. Their thought processes may be clouded by cognitive biases, such as confirmation bias, where they seek information that confirms their existing beliefs while dismissing or ignoring contradictory evidence. This leads to tunnel vision and a lack of openness to new perspectives and ideas.

Sloppy thinking also undermines effective communication and collaboration within teams and organizations. When leaders do not take the time to clarify their thoughts, consider alternative viewpoints, or communicate clearly, misunderstandings and conflicts can arise. Sloppy thinking can create an environment where assumptions go unchallenged, important information is overlooked, and team members feel undervalued or unheard.

Leaders who engage in sloppy thinking may struggle to recognize their own cognitive biases and blind spots. They may rely on simplistic or superficial reasoning, failing to delve deeper into complex issues and missing critical nuances. This can result in flawed strategies, ineffective problem-solving, and missed opportunities for growth and innovation.

To counter the impact of sloppy thinking, leaders must cultivate critical thinking skills and a commitment to intellectual rigor. They should actively seek diverse perspectives, encourage dissenting opinions, and promote a culture of open and honest dialogue. Leaders should also prioritize continuous learning and encourage their teams to engage in evidence-based decision-making, thorough analysis, and ongoing reflection. By fostering a culture of thoughtful and disciplined thinking, leaders can enhance their own decision-making capabilities and empower their teams to reach their full potential.

Sloppy thinking hampers effective leadership by limiting creativity, stifling innovation, and hindering problem-solving capabilities. Leaders who engage in sloppy thinking are prone to biased decision-making, closed-mindedness, and missed opportunities. By embracing critical thinking, intellectual rigor, and a commitment to ongoing learning, leaders can overcome the pitfalls of sloppy thinking and foster an environment of thoughtful and effective leadership.

KEY TAKEAWAY

3. Challenging Beliefs for Growth

Challenging beliefs for growth involves actively seeking out new information, perspectives, and experiences. Leaders should engage in continuous learning, both within and outside their areas of expertise, to broaden their knowledge and challenge preconceived notions. This could include attending conferences, reading diverse literature, participating in workshops or seminars, and seeking feedback from trusted mentors or colleagues.

Leaders should also foster a culture that encourages intellectual curiosity and the free exchange of ideas. They can create spaces for open dialogue, where team members feel comfortable sharing their thoughts and challenging existing beliefs. By actively listening and considering alternative viewpoints, leaders demonstrate a willingness to learn and grow, while also providing an opportunity for others to contribute their insights.

Leaders can encourage experimentation and risk-taking within their teams. By promoting an environment that embraces failure as a learning opportunity, leaders empower their team members to question assumptions, explore new approaches, and challenge the status quo.

Importantly, leaders must lead by example. They should openly acknowledge and share their own experiences of challenging beliefs and adapting their thinking. This vulnerability and transparency foster trust and create a culture where continuous learning and growth are valued.

KEY TAKEAWAY

Challenging beliefs for growth requires leaders to cultivate intellectual curiosity, embrace diverse perspectives, and create an environment that encourages open dialogue and experimentation. By continually questioning their own beliefs and seeking out new knowledge, leaders can overcome the limitations of sloppy thinking and foster a culture of continuous learning and growth within their teams and organizations.

---

4. Creating an Environment of Critical Thinking

Leaders have the responsibility to create an environment that fosters critical thinking and challenges sloppy thinking. They can encourage their team members to question assumptions, challenge the status quo, and seek alternative solutions. By promoting intellectual diversity and psychological safety, leaders empower their teams to contribute their unique perspectives and ideas.

Leaders can also cultivate a culture of continuous learning by providing opportunities for professional development, encouraging feedback, and modeling the behavior of critical thinking. By demonstrating a commitment to challenging their own beliefs and seeking input from others, leaders inspire their teams to adopt a similar mindset and embrace intellectual rigor.

Leaders can further foster critical thinking by implementing practices such as:

1. Encouraging inquiry: Leaders should create a safe space for team members to ask questions, voice concerns, and challenge existing ideas. They can promote a culture that values curiosity and rewards intellectual curiosity.

2. Promoting diverse perspectives: Leaders should actively seek out and include diverse perspectives in decision-making processes. This includes considering different backgrounds, experiences, and viewpoints, which can help identify blind spots and enhance the quality of decision-making.

3. Facilitating constructive debate: Leaders should encourage healthy debates and discussions where ideas are rigorously examined and evaluated. They can establish guidelines for respectful disagreement and provide opportunities for individuals to present alternative viewpoints and evidence.

4. Providing tools and resources: Leaders can equip their teams with the necessary tools and resources to enhance critical thinking skills. This can include training on logical reasoning, problem-solving techniques, and cognitive biases to help team members think more critically and objectively.

5. Recognizing and rewarding critical thinking: Leaders should recognize and reward individuals who demonstrate exceptional critical thinking skills. This can be done through performance evaluations, promotions, and public recognition, which reinforces the value of critical thinking within the organization.

6. *Embracing a growth mindset*: Leaders should foster a growth mindset culture that celebrates learning, resilience, and the willingness to challenge assumptions. By emphasizing the process of learning and improvement rather than solely focusing on outcomes, leaders inspire their teams to continuously develop their critical thinking abilities.

KEY TAKEAWAY

Leaders play a crucial role in creating an environment that nurtures critical thinking. By promoting inquiry, embracing diverse perspectives, facilitating constructive debate, providing tools and resources, recognizing critical thinking skills, and embracing a growth mindset, leaders can foster a culture of critical thinking that challenges sloppy thinking and drives innovation and excellence within their organizations.

Summary

Sloppy thinking can limit a leader's ability to create meaningful change and drive innovation within their teams and organizations. By recognizing the influence of beliefs and actively challenging them, leaders can overcome the constraints of their own thinking and foster an environment of critical thinking, intellectual curiosity, and innovation. By promoting a growth mindset and encouraging diverse perspectives, leaders empower their teams to create beyond the limitations of their beliefs, opening up new possibilities and driving sustainable success.

Leadership
KEY C●NCEPTS

10

A Leader Is a Ladder
Leaders Change from Who They Think They Are to Who They Truly Are

Introduction

The role of a leader goes beyond the external responsibilities and actions they undertake. True leadership involves a transformative journey of self-discovery and personal growth. Leaders have the opportunity to evolve and change from who they think they are to who they truly are. We will explore the concept of "Leader is a Ladder" and how leaders can embark on a transformative journey that aligns their authentic selves with their leadership roles.

1. Recognizing the Gap

Leaders who embark on the transformative journey of becoming their true selves recognize that there is a gap between who they think they are and who they truly are. This gap is often shaped by external factors such as societal expectations, cultural norms, and the pressures of leadership roles. Leaders may conform to these expectations, adopt a persona, or suppress aspects of their authentic selves to fit into predefined molds.

However, true leadership requires leaders to transcend these external influences and embrace their true essence. It necessitates a deep understanding and acceptance of their values, passions, strengths, and weaknesses. Leaders must recognize that their authentic selves are unique and bring value to their leadership roles. Embracing this understanding opens the door to personal growth, self-discovery, and the ability to lead with authenticity and integrity.

Self-reflection is a critical step in recognizing the gap between who leaders think they are and who they truly are. It involves introspection, questioning assumptions, and challenging long-held beliefs. Leaders must ask themselves profound questions about their motivations, aspirations, and values. They must be willing to confront their fears, vulnerabilities, and insecurities, which may have influenced their perceived identity.

This process of self-reflection requires leaders to detach themselves from external expectations and seek a deeper connection with their true selves. It involves exploring their passions, interests, and values, and aligning them with their leadership roles. Leaders may discover hidden talents, untapped potentials, or new perspectives that can significantly impact their approach to leadership.

Recognizing the gap between who leaders think they are and who they truly are is a powerful catalyst for personal transformation. It allows leaders to shed the limitations imposed by societal expectations and embrace their authentic selves. By bridging this gap, leaders can bring a genuine sense of purpose, passion, and commitment to their roles. They become more self-aware, empathetic, and capable of leading with integrity and authenticity.

Leaders who have recognized the gap and embarked on the journey of becoming their true selves inspire others to do the same. Their authenticity becomes a source of inspiration and motivation for their teams. By leading by example, they create an environment that values individuality, encourages self-expression, and fosters personal growth. This transformative journey not only benefits leaders themselves but also has a profound impact on the culture, performance, and success of their teams and organizations.

KEY TAKEAWAY

Recognizing the gap between who leaders think they are and who they truly are is a critical step in the transformative journey of leadership. By embracing their authentic selves, leaders can lead with integrity, purpose, and authenticity. They inspire others to do the same, fostering a culture of self-discovery, growth, and empowerment. Leaders who bridge this gap create a positive impact, not only within their organizations but also in society at large.

2. Self-Reflection and Self-Awareness

Self-reflection and self-awareness are indeed fundamental aspects of personal and leadership development. By engaging in introspection, leaders can gain a deeper understanding of themselves, which in turn enhances their ability to lead authentically. Here are some key points to consider regarding self-reflection and self-awareness in the context of becoming an authentic leader:

1. Understanding values: Self-reflection allows leaders to explore their core values and principles. Identifying and clarifying personal values helps leaders align their actions and decisions with what they hold to be most important. This alignment between values and actions enhances authenticity and fosters trust and respect from others.

2. Recognizing strengths and weaknesses: Self-awareness involves acknowledging both strengths and weaknesses. Leaders who are aware of their strengths can leverage them effectively, bringing out the best in themselves and their teams. Simultaneously, recognizing weaknesses allows leaders to seek development opportunities, delegate tasks wisely, and surround themselves with complementary skills.

3. Uncovering motivations: Self-reflection helps leaders understand their true motivations. This understanding enables them to align their goals and aspirations with their inner drives and passions. When leaders are driven by genuine motivations, they can inspire and influence others more effectively.

4. Developing emotional intelligence: Self-awareness is a cornerstone of emotional intelligence, which is crucial for effective leadership. By reflecting on their emotions, thoughts, and reactions, leaders can gain insights into how they impact their interactions with others. This awareness allows leaders to regulate their emotions and respond empathetically, fostering healthier relationships and better decision-making.

5. Building authenticity: Authentic leadership stems from a deep understanding of oneself. Through self-reflection, leaders can discover their authentic desires and motivations, enabling them to lead with integrity and genuine purpose. Authentic leaders are more relatable and trustworthy, as they stay true to themselves while inspiring and empowering others.

6. *Continuous growth and learning*: Self-reflection is an ongoing process that supports personal growth and learning. As leaders regularly reflect on their experiences, they can extract valuable lessons, adjust their approach, and refine their leadership style. This commitment to self-reflection demonstrates humility and a willingness to adapt, enhancing leadership effectiveness.

KEY TAKEAWAY

Self-reflection and self-awareness are crucial for leaders aiming to become authentic. By exploring their values, strengths, weaknesses, motivations, and aspirations, leaders gain a deeper understanding of themselves. This self-awareness forms the foundation for authentic leadership, enabling leaders to align their actions with their core values and lead with integrity and purpose.

3. Embracing Vulnerability

Embracing vulnerability is a transformative step in the journey of leaders as they change from who they think they are to who they truly are. Vulnerability involves being open, honest, and transparent about one's thoughts, emotions, and experiences. It requires leaders to let go of the fear of judgment, rejection, or failure and to embrace their authentic selves, even in moments of uncertainty or discomfort.

When leaders embrace vulnerability, they create an environment that encourages trust and psychological safety. By sharing their own vulnerabilities and challenges, leaders demonstrate humility and authenticity, allowing others to connect with them on a deeper level. This openness cultivates a culture of trust, where team members feel safe to express their ideas, concerns, and aspirations.

Vulnerability also fosters open communication within the team. When leaders are willing to show vulnerability, they encourage their team members to do the same. This openness leads to honest conversations, constructive feedback, and the sharing of diverse perspectives. As a result, teams become more collaborative, innovative, and resilient.

Furthermore, embracing vulnerability allows leaders to inspire and empower their teams. By showing their true selves, leaders become relatable and approachable. Team members feel comfortable seeking guidance and support, knowing that their leaders understand and empathize with their challenges. This vulnerability also humanizes leaders, making them more relatable and inspiring others to embrace their own vulnerabilities and take risks.

It's important to note that vulnerability does not mean being weak or passive. On the contrary, vulnerability requires strength, self-awareness, and the willingness to take calculated risks. Leaders who embrace vulnerability are not afraid to admit mistakes, acknowledge their limitations, and seek help when needed. They lead with humility and integrity, creating a culture where learning, growth, and resilience thrive.

> *Embracing vulnerability is an essential step for leaders to change from who they think they are to who they truly are. By embracing vulnerability, leaders create a culture of trust, open communication, and empowerment. They inspire others to embrace their own vulnerabilities, foster authenticity, and drive meaningful change within their teams and organizations. Through vulnerability, leaders create a space where individuals can bring their whole selves to work, contribute their unique talents, and achieve collective success.*

KEY TAKEAWAY

4. Developing Emotional Intelligence

Developing emotional intelligence is a vital aspect of a leader's journey to change from who they think they are to who they truly are. Emotional intelligence encompasses several key competencies that enable leaders to understand and manage their own emotions and effectively navigate relationships and interactions with others.

Firstly, self-awareness is essential for leaders to recognize their own emotions, strengths, weaknesses, and triggers. By developing self-awareness, leaders gain insight into their thoughts, feelings, and behaviors, allowing them to make conscious choices aligned with their true selves. Self-awareness also enables leaders to recognize the impact of their emotions on their decision-making and interactions with others.

Secondly, self-regulation involves the ability to manage and control one's emotions, impulses, and reactions. Leaders who can effectively regulate their emotions are better equipped to handle stress, remain composed in challenging situations, and make thoughtful decisions. They understand the importance of responding rather than reacting and are able to maintain emotional balance, even in high-pressure environments.

Empathy is another critical component of emotional intelligence. Leaders who develop empathy can understand and relate to the emotions and experiences of others. They actively listen, seek to understand different perspectives, and demonstrate genuine care and concern for their team members. Empathy fosters strong relationships, promotes collaboration, and enhances communication within the team.

Lastly, social skills encompass the ability to communicate effectively, build relationships, and influence others positively. Leaders with developed social skills can inspire, motivate, and empower their team members. They communicate their vision clearly, adapt their communication style to different individuals, and foster a culture of open dialogue and collaboration.

By developing emotional intelligence, leaders enhance their ability to connect with others authentically and lead with empathy and compassion. They create a supportive and inclusive environment where individuals feel valued, understood, and motivated to contribute their best work.

KEY TAKEAWAY

Developing emotional intelligence is an integral part of a leader's journey to change from who they think they are to who they truly are. By cultivating self-awareness, self-regulation, empathy, and social skills, leaders can lead with authenticity, empathy, and effectiveness. Emotionally intelligent leaders create a positive and empowering work environment, foster strong relationships, and drive meaningful change within their teams and organizations.

5. Aligning Values and Purpose

Leadership is not solely about holding a position or exercising authority; it is about embodying one's values and purpose. Effective leaders understand the importance of aligning their actions and decisions with their core values and defining a purpose that gives meaning to their leadership role. This alignment between values, purpose, and leadership is crucial in establishing authenticity, building trust, and inspiring others. This paper explores the significance of aligning values and purpose in leadership and its impact on creating meaningful and impactful leadership.

1. Identifying Core Values: Leadership that is aligned with one's values starts with the identification of core values. These values serve as a compass that guides leaders in their decision-making and actions. By understanding their values, leaders can prioritize what is most important to them and ensure that their behaviors and choices are in alignment with those values. Identifying core values helps leaders stay true to themselves and establish an authentic leadership style.

2. Defining Purpose: A clear sense of purpose is essential for leaders to make a meaningful impact. Purpose provides direction, motivation, and a sense of fulfillment. Leaders who have defined their purpose understand the impact they want to make and the contribution they want to bring to their teams, organizations, or communities. A defined purpose gives leaders a sense of meaning and guides their decisions and actions, ensuring they are aligned with their larger goals and aspirations.

3. Authenticity and Trust: Leaders who align their values and purpose with their leadership role are perceived as authentic and trustworthy. When leaders are consistent in their words, actions, and behaviors, it builds trust among their followers. People are more likely to trust and follow leaders who they perceive as genuine and true to themselves. By aligning values and purpose, leaders establish an authentic leadership presence that fosters trust and credibility.

4. Inspiring and Motivating Others: Leaders who align their values and purpose inspire and motivate others to do the same. When leaders are clear about their values and purpose, they can effectively communicate and inspire others to align their actions and decisions with their own values and purpose. This alignment creates a sense of shared purpose and a collective effort towards achieving common goals. Leaders become role models and catalysts for personal and professional growth.

5. Creating a Values-Driven Culture: Leaders who align their values and purpose have the opportunity to create a values-driven culture within their teams or organizations. They can establish norms and behaviors that reflect their core values, encouraging others to embrace and embody those values. A values-driven culture promotes unity, collaboration, and shared commitment towards a common purpose. It fosters an environment where individuals feel a sense of belonging and are motivated to contribute their best.

6. *Resilience and Adaptability*: Leaders who align their values and purpose are better equipped to navigate challenges and setbacks. When faced with difficult decisions or obstacles, leaders can rely on their values and purpose as a guiding light. This alignment provides a sense of clarity and resilience, enabling leaders to adapt and make choices that are in alignment with their core beliefs. It helps them stay focused and motivated even in challenging times.

KEY TAKEAWAY

Leadership that is aligned with values and purpose is authentic, inspiring, and impactful. By identifying core values and defining a clear purpose, leaders establish a solid foundation for their leadership journey. When leaders align their actions and decisions with their values and purpose, they create a sense of authenticity, build trust, and inspire others to do the same. They cultivate a values-driven culture and navigate challenges with resilience and adaptability. Aligning values and purpose allows leaders to make a meaningful impact and create positive change in their teams, organizations, and communities.

6. Continuous Growth and Learning

Continuous growth and learning are essential elements of a leader's journey to change from who they think they are to who they truly are. Leaders who commit to ongoing personal and professional development demonstrate a growth mindset—an attitude that embraces challenges, seeks opportunities for learning, and values continuous improvement.

Leaders can engage in various activities to foster continuous growth and learning. They can attend leadership development programs, workshops, or conferences to gain new insights and perspectives. They can also pursue formal education, such as earning advanced degrees or certifications, to deepen their knowledge in specific areas.

Additionally, leaders can seek out mentors or coaches who can provide guidance, support, and valuable feedback. Engaging in regular self-reflection and self-assessment allows leaders to identify areas for improvement and set goals for their development.

Leaders should actively seek diverse experiences and challenges that push them out of their comfort zones. By taking on new responsibilities, leading cross-functional projects, or embracing roles outside their expertise, leaders broaden their skills, enhance their adaptability, and strengthen their leadership capabilities.

Importantly, continuous growth and learning involve not only acquiring new knowledge and skills but also integrating and applying them in practical settings. Leaders should strive to translate their learning into action, incorporating new insights and approaches into their leadership practices.

By committing to continuous growth and learning, leaders cultivate a growth mindset that fuels their personal and professional development. They become adaptable, innovative, and resilient, capable of navigating complex challenges and driving meaningful change. Continuous growth and learning enable leaders to stay ahead in a rapidly evolving world, inspire their teams, and create a culture of continuous improvement and excellence.

> *Continuous growth and learning are fundamental to the journey of becoming an authentic leader. Leaders who embrace a growth mindset and actively seek out opportunities for development enhance their leadership capabilities, adaptability, and effectiveness. By committing to continuous growth and learning, leaders inspire their teams and organizations to thrive in a dynamic and ever-changing world.*

KEY TAKEAWAY

7. Inspiring and Empowering Others

Leaders who have undergone a personal transformation from who they think they are to who they truly are have the ability to inspire and empower others. Their authentic leadership style, rooted in self-awareness and a deep understanding of their values, creates an environment that encourages and uplifts individuals.

By embracing their true selves, leaders become role models for authenticity and integrity. They demonstrate the importance of living in alignment with one's values and beliefs, inspiring others to do the same. Their ability to show vulnerability and share personal experiences creates a sense of connection and relatability, fostering trust and rapport with their team members.

Authentic leaders also possess a genuine interest in the growth and development of their team members. They take the time to understand their strengths, aspirations, and challenges, providing support and guidance to help individuals reach their full potential. By empowering others, leaders create a sense of ownership and accountability, enabling individuals to take initiative and make meaningful contributions.

Leaders who have changed from who they think they are to who they truly are demonstrate empathy and compassion. They create a safe space where individuals feel heard, understood, and valued. This fosters a culture of inclusivity, collaboration, and psychological safety, encouraging open communication and the sharing of diverse perspectives.

Through their authentic leadership, these leaders inspire a shared vision and purpose. They communicate their values, aspirations, and expectations clearly, aligning their teams toward a common goal. This shared vision creates a sense of belonging and unity, motivating individuals to work collaboratively and strive for excellence.

KEY TAKEAWAY

Leaders who have changed from who they think they are to who they truly are have the power to inspire and empower others. Their authenticity, empathy, and ability to create a shared vision foster a culture of trust, collaboration, and personal growth. By embracing their true selves and leading with integrity, these leaders become catalysts for positive change and transformation within their teams and organizations.

Summary

The journey of a leader is a transformative process that involves changing from who they think they are to who they truly are. By engaging in self-reflection, embracing vulnerability, developing emotional intelligence, aligning values and purpose, committing to continuous growth, and inspiring and empowering others, leaders can become authentic leaders who make a profound impact on their teams and organizations. Embracing this transformative journey enables leaders to reach their full potential and create a positive and lasting legacy.

Leadership
KEY CONCEPTS

11

What You Don't Fix the Kids Inherit
Leaders Break the Paradigm Cycle

Introduction

In the world of leadership, there exists a cycle that often perpetuates outdated paradigms and stifles progress. This cycle can be observed in various aspects of society, including education, business, and social norms. However, true leaders understand the importance of breaking free from this cycle and challenging the status quo. They recognize that what we don't fix, the next generation inherits, and they are committed to creating a new paradigm that fosters growth, innovation, and positive change.

1. Understanding the Paradigm Cycle

The paradigm cycle is a phenomenon that affects various aspects of society, including education, business, and social norms. It describes the tendency for beliefs, behaviors, and systems to be passed down from one generation to another without undergoing critical examination. This perpetuation of established norms can limit progress and hinder innovation. However, leaders who possess a visionary mindset understand the importance of breaking free from the paradigm cycle and driving transformative change. They recognize that blindly following tradition and adhering to outdated practices stifles growth and inhibits the development of new ideas and perspectives.

The Impact of the Paradigm Cycle

The paradigm cycle has significant implications for leadership and organizational development. When leaders succumb to the cycle, they become entrenched in conventional thinking and resist change. They may rely on outdated models and approaches that no longer align with the evolving needs of their organizations and stakeholders. As a result, they unintentionally perpetuate the status quo and hinder progress and innovation.

Breaking the Paradigm Cycle

Leaders who aspire to break the paradigm cycle understand that true progress requires challenging the established norms and belief systems. They recognize that blindly following tradition can lead to stagnation and missed opportunities for growth and improvement. These leaders possess a visionary mindset and have the courage to question existing paradigms, challenge assumptions, and seek out new possibilities.

Promoting Critical Examination

To break the paradigm cycle, leaders must promote critical examination of existing beliefs and behaviors. They encourage their teams to question why things are done a certain way and explore alternative approaches. By fostering an environment of intellectual curiosity and open dialogue, leaders create opportunities for fresh perspectives, innovative thinking, and creative problem-solving.

Embracing Diversity of Thought

Leaders who aim to break the paradigm cycle understand the value of diversity of thought. They actively seek out and embrace different perspectives, recognizing that diverse voices can offer unique insights and challenge the status quo. By creating an inclusive environment where individuals feel safe to express their opinions, leaders encourage the exploration of new ideas and foster a culture of innovation and growth.

Encouraging Experimentation and Risk-Taking

Breaking the paradigm cycle requires leaders to foster a culture that values experimentation and risk-taking. They create an atmosphere where individuals feel empowered to test new ideas, learn from failures, and adapt their approaches. These leaders understand that innovation often arises from taking calculated risks and embracing the potential for growth that comes with stepping outside of the comfort zone.

Leading by Example

Leaders who break the paradigm cycle lead by example. They demonstrate the courage to challenge existing norms and exhibit a willingness to embrace change. By embodying a growth mindset and displaying a willingness to learn and adapt, they inspire their teams to do the same. These leaders become catalysts for transformative change and create a ripple effect throughout their organizations.

Breaking the paradigm cycle is crucial for leaders who seek to drive transformative change and foster innovation within their organizations. By promoting critical examination, embracing diversity of thought, encouraging experimentation and risk-taking, and leading by example, leaders can overcome the limitations of established norms and create a culture of continuous improvement and growth. In doing so, they unlock the potential for fresh ideas, novel approaches, and meaningful progress, ensuring that their organizations remain agile, adaptive, and successful in an ever-evolving world.

KEY TAKEAWAY

2. Challenging the Status Quo

In a rapidly changing world, leaders who break the paradigm cycle are essential for driving progress and innovation. These leaders understand that sticking to the status quo stifles growth and limits the potential for transformation. Instead, they have a strong desire to challenge existing beliefs, assumptions, and systems. By encouraging critical thinking, fostering a culture of innovation, and challenging the status quo, these leaders create an environment that embraces change and propels organizations forward.

Questioning Long-Held Traditions

Leaders who disrupt the status quo are not afraid to question long-held traditions and conventional wisdom. They recognize that what worked in the past may not be relevant or effective in the present or future. These leaders challenge the assumptions underlying established practices and encourage their teams to think critically and explore new approaches. By questioning the status quo, leaders open up opportunities for fresh perspectives, creative solutions, and breakthrough innovations.

Embracing New Possibilities

Effective leaders have a mindset that embraces new possibilities and are not constrained by preconceived notions or limited thinking. These leaders encourage their teams to think outside the box, explore uncharted territories, and challenge boundaries. They foster a culture that values curiosity, experimentation, and calculated risk-taking. By embracing new possibilities, leaders inspire their teams to push beyond limitations and discover innovative ways to solve problems and achieve goals.

Fostering a Culture of Innovation

Leaders who disrupt the paradigm cycle understand the importance of fostering a culture of innovation within their organizations. They create an environment where creativity is encouraged, ideas are valued, and diverse perspectives are welcomed. These leaders empower their teams to challenge the status quo, experiment with new approaches, and learn from failures. They provide the necessary resources and support for innovation to thrive, whether it's through dedicated innovation programs, cross-functional collaborations, or open communication channels.

Encouraging Critical Thinking

Leaders that are able to break the paradigm loop prioritize critical thinking. They encourage their teams to question assumptions, challenge established norms, and seek evidence-based solutions. These leaders create an atmosphere where intellectual curiosity is nurtured, and diverse opinions are respected. They promote the habit of asking thought-provoking questions, analyzing problems from different angles, and seeking out new information. By encouraging critical thinking, leaders foster an environment that values intellectual rigor and ensures that decisions are based on careful analysis rather than complacency.

Challenging the Status Quo

Leaders understand that progress requires challenging the status quo. They recognize that clinging to outdated practices and beliefs hinders growth and innovation. These leaders are not satisfied with mediocrity or maintaining the same old routines. Instead, they actively seek out opportunities for improvement and disruption. They encourage their teams to challenge assumptions, propose alternative solutions, and embrace change. By challenging the status quo, leaders create a culture of continuous improvement and drive organizations to reach new heights.

> Leaders who break the paradigm cycle have a transformative impact on their organizations and the broader landscape. By questioning long-held traditions, embracing new possibilities, fostering a culture of innovation, encouraging critical thinking, and challenging the status quo, these leaders create an environment that thrives on growth, innovation, and success. They inspire their teams to push beyond boundaries, unlock their full potential, and achieve extraordinary results. In a world that is constantly evolving, leaders who break the paradigm cycle are indispensable for driving progress and shaping a brighter future.

KEY TAKEAWAY

3. Fostering a Culture of Continuous Improvement

In a dynamic and rapidly changing world, fostering a culture of continuous improvement is crucial for organizations to thrive. Leaders who break the paradigm cycle understand the significance of embracing change, challenging the status quo, and constantly seeking better ways of doing things. By nurturing a culture of continuous improvement, these leaders create an environment where innovation, learning, and growth flourish.

Embracing a Growth Mindset

Leaders who foster a culture of continuous improvement embrace a growth mindset. They believe that individuals and organizations have the capacity to learn, adapt, and improve over time. These leaders encourage their teams to view challenges and setbacks as opportunities for growth rather than obstacles. By promoting a growth mindset, leaders inspire a sense of curiosity, resilience, and a willingness to learn from mistakes and feedback.

Encouraging Innovation and Experimentation

A culture of continuous improvement encourages innovation and experimentation. Leaders create an environment where individuals are encouraged to generate new ideas, take calculated risks, and test novel approaches. They support and reward individuals who are willing to challenge the status quo and propose innovative solutions. By fostering a spirit of innovation and experimentation, leaders empower their teams to think creatively, explore new possibilities, and find better ways to achieve organizational goals.

Promoting Learning and Development

Leaders foster a culture of continuous improvement and prioritize learning and development. They provide resources and opportunities for individuals to acquire new skills, knowledge, and perspectives. These leaders encourage their teams to seek out learning experiences, whether through training programs, workshops, or self-directed learning. By promoting a learning culture, leaders ensure that individuals are equipped with the necessary tools and capabilities to adapt to changing circumstances and drive improvement.

Embracing Feedback and Reflection

Continuous improvement requires a willingness to receive feedback and engage in self-reflection. Leaders who foster a culture of continuous improvement create an environment where individuals feel safe and encouraged to provide feedback, share insights, and engage in open dialogue. These leaders actively seek feedback from their teams and use it as a valuable source of information for growth and improvement. They also encourage individuals to engage in self-reflection, encouraging them to assess their own performance, identify areas for improvement, and set goals for personal and professional development.

Recognizing and Celebrating Progress

Leaders who promote a culture of continual improvement recognize and celebrate progress. They acknowledge and appreciate the efforts and achievements of individuals and teams in their pursuit of excellence. By celebrating progress, leaders reinforce the importance of continuous improvement and motivate their teams to sustain their commitment to growth. They also use progress as an opportunity to inspire further innovation and reinforce the culture of continuous improvement.

KEY TAKEAWAY

4. Encouraging Creativity and Risk-Taking

In a continually changing and competitive corporate environment, leaders who break the paradigm cycle recognize the importance of encouraging creativity and risk-taking. They understand that innovation and growth often arise from thinking outside the box and taking calculated risks. By fostering a culture that embraces creativity and risk-taking, these leaders empower their teams to explore new possibilities, challenge existing norms, and drive meaningful change.

Creating a Safe Environment for Ideas

Leaders who encourage creativity and risk-taking create a safe and supportive environment for individuals to share their ideas. They foster open communication, actively listen to diverse perspectives, and value contributions from all team members. By creating a culture of psychological safety, leaders ensure that individuals feel comfortable expressing their ideas, even if they deviate from conventional thinking. This fosters a sense of trust, collaboration, and empowerment, laying the foundation for creative thinking and innovation.

Promoting a Growth Mindset

Leaders who break the paradigm cycle promote a growth mindset within their teams. They believe that abilities and skills can be developed through dedication, effort, and learning. By encouraging their teams to embrace challenges, persist in the face of setbacks, and view failure as an opportunity for growth, leaders cultivate a mindset that fosters creativity and risk-taking. They emphasize the importance of continuous learning, experimentation, and embracing new experiences as pathways to personal and professional development.

Supporting Experimentation and Learning from Failure

Leaders who encourage risk-taking understand that failure is an inherent part of the innovation process. They provide their teams with the necessary resources, autonomy, and support to experiment and try new approaches. These leaders foster a culture that views failure as a valuable learning opportunity rather than a negative outcome. They encourage individuals to reflect on their failures, extract valuable insights, and apply them to future endeavors. By promoting a mindset that embraces learning from failure, leaders inspire their teams to take calculated risks and push the boundaries of what is possible.

Celebrating and Rewarding Innovation

Leaders recognize and celebrate innovative thinking and outcomes. They create a system of recognition and rewards that reinforces the importance of creativity and risk-taking. These leaders publicly acknowledge and appreciate individuals and teams for their innovative ideas, successful initiatives, and breakthrough achievements. By celebrating innovation, leaders create a culture where creativity is valued and individuals feel motivated to explore new possibilities and contribute their best work.

Leading by Example

Leaders who break the paradigm cycle lead by example when it comes to encouraging creativity and risk-taking. They demonstrate their own openness to new ideas, their willingness to take calculated risks, and their ability to learn from failure. By modeling the behaviors and attitudes they seek from their teams, leaders inspire others to embrace creativity, think outside the box, and take calculated risks. Through their own actions, leaders create a ripple effect that encourages innovative thinking and risk-taking throughout the organization.

5. Leading by Example:

In today's fast-paced world, leaders who break the paradigm cycle understand the importance of leading by example. They recognize that their actions speak louder than words and that they have the power to inspire and influence others through their own behaviors and attitudes. By embodying the courage, resilience, and adaptability needed to challenge the status quo, these leaders set a powerful example for their teams and organizations to follow.

Modeling Courage and Resilience

Leaders model courage and resilience in the face of adversity. They demonstrate the willingness to take calculated risks, step outside of their comfort zones, and confront the unknown. These leaders understand that change and innovation require courage and are not deterred by potential setbacks or failures. By displaying their own courage and resilience, leaders inspire others to embrace challenges, overcome obstacles, and push through barriers in pursuit of meaningful change.

Embracing Change and Adaptability

Change and adaptation are essential characteristics for leaders. They recognize that the world is constantly evolving, and staying stagnant is not an option. These leaders proactively seek out new ideas, technologies, and approaches, and are open to adjusting their strategies and plans based on new information. By demonstrating their own willingness to change and adapt, leaders create a culture of continuous improvement and innovation within their organizations.

Demonstrating Integrity and Ethical Behavior

Leaders demonstrate integrity and ethical behavior in all aspects of their leadership. They consistently act in alignment with their values, setting a standard of honesty, transparency, and accountability. These leaders prioritize the greater good over personal gain and make decisions that are ethically sound and morally principled. By upholding high standards of integrity, leaders inspire trust, respect, and loyalty among their teams and stakeholders.

Encouraging Collaboration and Teamwork

Leaders understand the importance of collaboration and teamwork. They foster an inclusive and supportive environment where diverse perspectives are valued and everyone feels empowered to contribute their best. These leaders actively promote collaboration, break down silos, and encourage cross-functional teamwork. By fostering a culture of collaboration, leaders create an environment where innovation thrives and collective intelligence is harnessed.

Promoting Continuous Learning and Growth

Leaders are committed to their own continuous learning and growth. They invest in their personal and professional development, seeking out new knowledge, skills, and experiences. These leaders encourage and support the growth and development of their teams, providing opportunities for learning, mentorship, and skill-building. By demonstrating a commitment to continuous learning, leaders inspire their teams to embrace a growth mindset and strive for ongoing improvement.

KEY TAKEAWAY

Leading by example is a powerful tool for leaders who seek to break the paradigm cycle. By modeling courage, adaptability, integrity, collaboration, and a commitment to continuous learning, leaders inspire their teams and organizations to challenge the status quo, embrace change, and drive meaningful transformation. Through their actions and behaviors, these leaders create a culture of innovation, resilience, and growth, propelling their organizations forward in an ever-changing world.

6. Creating a Legacy of Transformation

Leaders who break the paradigm cycle leave a lasting legacy of transformation. By challenging the outdated paradigms of the past, they create new possibilities for future generations. These leaders pave the way for progress, innovation, and positive change, ensuring that what we don't fix is not inherited by the next generation. They establish a new paradigm that promotes continuous improvement, critical thinking, and a commitment to creating a better future.

These leaders inspire others to question the status quo, challenge their own beliefs, and embrace the courage to create change. By breaking the paradigm cycle, they empower individuals to think differently, explore new ideas, and find innovative solutions to complex problems. Their legacy is one of transformation, where organizations and communities thrive in an environment that values growth, adaptability, and the pursuit of excellence.

Leaders foster a culture of empowerment and ownership. They encourage individuals to take initiative, think creatively, and take responsibility for their actions. By nurturing a sense of ownership and accountability, these leaders cultivate a workforce that is driven to make a positive impact and contribute to the organization's success.

In addition, leaders who break the paradigm cycle understand the importance of succession planning and mentoring the next generation of leaders. They invest in developing future leaders who share their vision, values, and commitment to transformative change. By mentoring and guiding emerging leaders, they ensure the continuity of their legacy and inspire a new wave of paradigm breakers.

Ultimately, leaders who break the paradigm cycle understand that the true measure of their success lies in the positive impact they leave behind. They create a ripple effect of transformation that extends far beyond their own tenure, shaping the future of their organizations, industries, and even society as a whole.

KEY TAKEAWAY

Leaders who break the paradigm cycle are catalysts for transformation. Through their courageous actions, commitment to continuous improvement, and empowerment of others, they challenge the status quo and create a legacy of positive change. By inspiring individuals to think differently, embrace innovation, and pursue excellence, these leaders leave a lasting impact on their organizations and communities. Their efforts ensure that what we don't fix is not inherited by future generations, but rather replaced by a new paradigm of growth, adaptability, and continuous transformation.

Summary

Leaders who break the paradigm cycle understand the significance of challenging the status quo and driving transformative change. They recognize that what we don't fix is inherited by the next generation, and they are committed to breaking this cycle to create a better future. By fostering a culture of continuous improvement, encouraging creativity and risk-taking, and leading by example, these leaders shape a new paradigm that promotes growth, innovation, and positive change. They leave a lasting legacy of transformation, ensuring a brighter future for generations to come.

Leadership
KEY C⦿NCEPTS

12

Gratitude Is Faith in Action
Leaders Act With Unconditional Love

Introduction

Leadership is not just about achieving goals and driving performance; it is also about the values and principles that guide one's actions. Gratitude and unconditional love are two essential qualities that set exceptional leaders apart. When leaders embrace gratitude and act with unconditional love, they create an environment of compassion, appreciation, and support. We will explore the concept that gratitude is faith in action and how leaders can incorporate unconditional love into their leadership approach.

1. The Power of Gratitude

Acting with unconditional love means embodying empathy, compassion, and kindness towards others. It transcends personal biases, judgments, and expectations. Leaders who act with unconditional love genuinely care about the well-being and growth of their team members, inspiring them to reach their full potential. They create a culture where mistakes are seen as opportunities for learning, and failures are met with understanding and encouragement.

When leaders integrate gratitude and unconditional love into their leadership approach, they create a harmonious and transformative environment. They express gratitude for the unique talents, strengths, and contributions of their team members, inspiring a sense of belonging and purpose. Simultaneously, leaders act with unconditional love by showing understanding, compassion, and support during challenging times. They foster a culture of psychological safety and create an atmosphere where individuals can flourish and unleash their full potential.

Leaders who embrace gratitude and act with unconditional love experience several positive outcomes within their organizations. They build strong relationships based on trust, authenticity, and mutual respect. Team members feel seen, heard, and appreciated, resulting in increased engagement, motivation, and loyalty. Leaders who lead with gratitude and unconditional love inspire a sense of belonging and purpose, leading to higher levels of job satisfaction, well-being, and overall organizational performance.

KEY TAKEAWAY

Gratitude and unconditional love are powerful qualities that leaders can cultivate to create a positive and transformative leadership approach. By expressing gratitude and acting with unconditional love towards their team members, leaders foster an environment of positivity, resilience, and fulfillment. This approach inspires a sense of purpose, motivation, and loyalty, leading to higher levels of engagement, well-being, and organizational success. Ultimately, leaders who practice gratitude and act with unconditional love make a profound and lasting impact on individuals, organizations, and society as a whole.

2. Gratitude as Faith in Action

Acting with unconditional love means embodying empathy, compassion, and kindness towards others. It transcends personal biases, judgments, and expectations. Leaders who act with unconditional love genuinely care about the well-being and growth of their team members, inspiring them to reach their full potential. They create a culture where mistakes are seen as opportunities for learning, and failures are met with understanding and encouragement.

When leaders integrate gratitude and unconditional love into their leadership approach, they create a harmonious and transformative environment. They express gratitude for the unique talents, strengths, and contributions of their team members, inspiring a sense of belonging and purpose. Simultaneously, leaders act with unconditional love by showing understanding, compassion, and support during challenging times. They foster a culture of psychological safety and create an atmosphere where individuals can flourish and unleash their full potential.

Leaders who embrace gratitude and act with unconditional love experience several positive outcomes within their organizations. They build strong relationships based on trust, authenticity, and mutual respect. Team members feel seen, heard, and appreciated, resulting in increased engagement, motivation, and loyalty. Leaders who lead with gratitude and unconditional love inspire a sense of belonging and purpose, leading to higher levels of job satisfaction, well-being, and overall organizational performance.

KEY TAKEAWAY

Gratitude and unconditional love are powerful qualities that leaders can cultivate to create a positive and transformative leadership approach. By expressing gratitude and acting with unconditional love towards their team members, leaders foster an environment of positivity, resilience, and fulfillment. This approach inspires a sense of purpose, motivation, and loyalty, leading to higher levels of engagement, well-being, and organizational success. Ultimately, leaders who practice gratitude and act with unconditional love make a profound and lasting impact on individuals, organizations, and society as a whole.

3. Acting with Unconditional Love

Leaders who act with unconditional love go beyond superficial interactions and develop deep connections with their team members. They actively listen, seek to understand, and validate the feelings and experiences of others. They demonstrate empathy by putting themselves in the shoes of their team members and considering their perspectives and emotions.

By acting with unconditional love, leaders create an environment where individuals feel safe to take risks, express their ideas, and be vulnerable. This fosters creativity, innovation, and collaboration, as team members are empowered to contribute their unique perspectives and talents. Leaders who lead with unconditional love cultivate a sense of trust and loyalty among their team members, creating a cohesive and high-performing team.

Leaders who act with unconditional love embody a servant leadership mindset. They prioritize the needs of their team members above their own, supporting their growth and well-being. They actively engage in mentoring, coaching, and providing opportunities for development. By investing in the personal and professional growth of their team members, leaders create a culture of continuous learning and improvement.

KEY TAKEAWAY

Leaders who act with unconditional love create a transformative and compassionate leadership style. They cultivate an environment of psychological safety, trust, and collaboration. By demonstrating empathy, compassion, and kindness, leaders inspire their team members to reach their full potential and contribute their best. This approach not only enhances individual well-being and growth but also leads to higher levels of engagement, productivity, and overall organizational success. Leaders who act with unconditional love make a profound and lasting impact on the lives of their team members and create a positive and inclusive work environment.

4. The Integration of Gratitude and Unconditional Love

Through the integration of gratitude and unconditional love, leaders establish deep connections and build trust among their team members. They demonstrate their genuine care and concern for the well-being and growth of each individual. This creates an environment where team members feel valued, appreciated, and motivated to give their best.

Leaders who embrace gratitude and unconditional love also cultivate a positive and inclusive work culture. They encourage collaboration, open communication, and a sense of community. By valuing diversity and embracing different perspectives, these leaders foster innovation and creativity within their teams. They create an atmosphere where everyone feels heard, respected, and empowered to contribute their unique ideas and talents.

When leading with gratitude and unconditional love, leaders inspire a sense of purpose and meaning in their team members. They connect the work being done to a larger vision and encourage a focus on the positive impact created. This helps individuals find fulfillment and satisfaction in their work, leading to increased engagement and productivity.

5. The Impact of Gratitude and Unconditional Love:

Leaders who embrace gratitude and act with unconditional love create a culture of support and collaboration. They foster an environment where team members feel safe to take risks, share ideas, and learn from their mistakes. This promotes innovation, creativity, and continuous improvement within the organization.

In addition, leaders who practice gratitude and unconditional love have a positive impact on the overall well-being of their team members. They prioritize the holistic development of individuals, considering their personal and professional growth. By showing empathy, compassion, and understanding, leaders contribute to the overall happiness and fulfillment of their team members, resulting in reduced stress, increased resilience, and improved work-life balance.

Leaders who embody gratitude and unconditional love serve as role models for their teams. Their actions and behaviors inspire others to adopt similar attitudes and approaches, creating a ripple effect throughout the organization. This leads to a positive and uplifting work culture, characterized by kindness, collaboration, and a shared commitment to collective success.

Summary

Gratitude is faith in action, and leaders who act with unconditionallovecreateatransformativeandcompassionate environment. By embracing gratitude, leaders inspire positivity, resilience, and a culture of appreciation. Through unconditional love, leaders foster empathy, compassion, and support for their team members. When leaders integrate these qualities into their leadership approach, they create a meaningful and fulfilling experience for themselves and their teams. Ultimately, leaders who practice gratitude and act with unconditional love make a profound and lasting impact on individuals, organizations, and society as a whole.

Leadership

KEY C(I)NCEPTS

13

Dig the Ditches
Leaders Expect Around the Reality That Has Their Attention

Introduction

In the world of leadership, the ability to perceive and understand reality accurately is essential. However, great leaders understand that reality is not fixed and can be influenced by their expectations and mindset. Leaders who embrace the concept of "Dig The Ditches" recognize that they have the power to shape their reality by expecting and planning for the outcomes they desire. We will explore the idea that leaders can expect around the reality that has their attention, enabling them to overcome challenges, drive success, and inspire their teams.

1. Perceiving Reality

Perceiving reality accurately is a fundamental aspect of effective leadership. Great leaders understand the importance of assessing the current situation, gathering relevant information, and identifying the challenges and opportunities that lie ahead. They do not shy away from acknowledging potential limitations or obstacles that may exist.

However, what sets great leaders apart is their ability to transcend the limitations of the present reality. They refuse to be confined by the circumstances and constraints that may be apparent.

Instead, they shift their focus to what they can create and expect, even in the face of obstacles.

By adopting this mindset, leaders open themselves up to new possibilities and opportunities. They recognize that their expectations and beliefs shape their reality. They understand that by expecting more and aiming higher, they can inspire their teams and drive meaningful change.

Leaders who expect around the reality cultivate a mindset of possibility and resilience. They envision a future that surpasses the limitations of the present circumstances. This mindset fuels their creativity, innovation, and problem-solving abilities. They approach challenges with optimism, seeing them as opportunities for growth and improvement.

Leaders who expect around the reality inspire and motivate their teams to do the same. They create a culture of possibility, where individuals are encouraged to think beyond the status quo and pursue ambitious goals. By setting high expectations and fostering a climate of innovation and continuous improvement, leaders empower their teams to strive for greatness.

It is important to note that expecting around the reality does not mean denying or ignoring the challenges that exist. Great leaders maintain a realistic understanding of the current situation and take strategic actions to address the obstacles they face. They combine their visionary mindset with strategic planning, effective communication, and proactive decision-making to navigate the complexities of the real world.

KEY TAKEAWAY

Leaders who perceive reality accurately and expect around it have the power to create meaningful change. By refusing to be confined by the present circumstances, they inspire their teams to embrace possibility, foster innovation, and drive success. Through their visionary mindset, they shape a future that goes beyond the limitations of the current reality, creating a positive impact on their organizations and the people they lead.

2. Expecting Around the Reality

Expecting around the reality is a powerful leadership mindset that enables leaders to transcend the constraints of the present and envision a future that surpasses what may seem possible. Leaders who dig the ditches understand that the current reality is not a fixed state, but rather a starting point from which they can create and shape their desired outcomes.

By expecting beyond the limitations of the current reality, leaders tap into their creative potential and cultivate a mindset of possibility. They challenge conventional thinking, question existing paradigms, and explore innovative solutions. Instead of being deterred by obstacles, they view them as opportunities for growth and learning.

Leaders who expect around the reality inspire their teams to think bigger and aim higher. They communicate their vision with clarity and passion, igniting a sense of purpose and excitement among their team members. By setting high expectations and fostering a culture of continuous improvement, leaders empower their teams to stretch their capabilities and achieve extraordinary results.

Expecting leaders demonstrate resilience in the face of setbacks and adversity. They do not allow temporary setbacks to dampen their spirits or derail their progress. Instead, they view challenges as temporary roadblocks that can be overcome with perseverance and determination.

By modeling a mindset of expectation and resilience, leaders create a ripple effect within their organizations. They inspire their teams to embrace a growth mindset, take calculated risks, and persist in the pursuit of their goals. This culture of expectation and resilience fuels innovation, fosters collaboration, and drives organizational success.

It is important to note that expecting around the reality does not imply ignoring or denying the current challenges or limitations. Leaders remain grounded in reality and recognize the importance of strategic planning, adaptability, and effective execution. They balance their visionary mindset with a practical approach, aligning their expectations with thoughtful action.

Leaders who expect around the reality have the ability to transform their organizations and achieve extraordinary results. By envisioning a future beyond the constraints of the current reality, they inspire innovation, resilience, and growth. Through their visionary mindset and ability to set high expectations, leaders create a culture of possibility and empower their teams to reach new heights.

KEY
TAKEAWAY

---

3. Planning and Preparation

Planning and preparation are essential components of expecting around the reality. Leaders who dig the ditches recognize that setting high expectations requires a strategic approach to turn those expectations into reality. They understand that a well-thought-out plan provides a roadmap for success and helps navigate potential challenges.

Effective planning involves a thorough assessment of the current reality, including an understanding of the strengths, weaknesses, opportunities, and threats. Leaders gather relevant information, analyze data, and seek input from key stakeholders to inform their planning process. By considering various perspectives and insights, leaders can develop a comprehensive and realistic plan that accounts for the complexities of the situation.

In addition to assessing the current reality, leaders who dig the ditches engage in forward-thinking. They envision the desired outcome and set specific, measurable, achievable, relevant, and time-bound (SMART) goals. This allows them to clearly define the path and milestones necessary to reach their expectations.

With a solid plan in place, leaders allocate resources effectively and identify the actions required to execute the plan. They delegate tasks, empower their team members, and provide the necessary support and guidance. By ensuring that each individual understands their role and responsibilities, leaders foster a sense of ownership and accountability within the team.

Leaders who dig the ditches proactively anticipate potential obstacles and develop contingency plans. They consider alternative scenarios and develop strategies to address unexpected challenges. This proactive approach enables leaders and their teams to navigate obstacles more effectively and stay on track towards their expectations.

Throughout the planning and preparation process, effective communication plays a vital role. Leaders ensure that their expectations, goals, and plans are clearly communicated to all relevant stakeholders. This fosters alignment, commitment, and collaboration, as everyone understands their role in achieving the shared vision.

4. Inspiring and Motivating Others

Leaders who expect around the reality have a profound impact on their teams. Their unwavering belief in what is possible inspires and motivates others to reach higher and push beyond their perceived limitations. By setting high expectations, leaders create a culture of excellence, innovation, and continuous improvement. They empower their teams to challenge the status quo and strive for greatness.

Through their own example, leaders demonstrate the possibilities that can be achieved by expecting around the reality. They model the behaviors, attitudes, and work ethic that align with their high expectations. This inspires their team members to step out of their comfort zones, embrace new challenges, and strive for personal and professional growth.

Leaders who expect around the reality understand the importance of effective communication. They articulate their expectations clearly and provide a compelling vision that resonates with their team members. They communicate the value and significance of the work they are doing, instilling a sense of purpose and meaning in their teams.

Expecting leaders empower their teams by providing the necessary support and resources to succeed. They invest in their team members' development, provide opportunities for learning and growth, and remove obstacles that may hinder progress. By creating an environment of trust and psychological safety, leaders foster a sense of ownership and autonomy, enabling their team members to excel.

Leaders who expect around the reality also celebrate and recognize achievements along the way. They acknowledge and appreciate the efforts and accomplishments of their team members, reinforcing a positive and motivating work environment. This recognition reinforces the belief that their expectations are attainable and that their hard work is valued.

KEY TAKEAWAY

Leaders who expect around the reality have the power to inspire and motivate their teams to reach higher levels of performance. Through their unwavering belief in what is possible and their commitment to setting high expectations, they create a culture of excellence, innovation, and continuous improvement. By modeling the behaviors they expect from others, providing support and resources, and recognizing achievements, leaders empower their teams to exceed their own expectations and achieve extraordinary results.

5. Adaptability and Agility

Adaptability and agility are essential traits for leaders who expect around the reality. They understand that the path to success is rarely a straight line and that circumstances may change along the way. These leaders are able to quickly assess new information, adjust their expectations, and pivot their plans accordingly.

By embracing adaptability, leaders demonstrate resilience and resourcefulness. They are not deterred by setbacks or unexpected obstacles. Instead, they view them as learning opportunities and leverage them to find alternative solutions and approaches.

One of the key characteristics of adaptable leaders is their resilience. They understand that setbacks and obstacles are inevitable in any endeavor. Rather than being discouraged or disheartened, they view these challenges as valuable learning opportunities. They analyze the situation, identify what went wrong, and extract lessons that can inform future decisions and actions. Through their resilience, leaders bounce back from setbacks stronger and more determined to succeed.

In addition to resilience, adaptable leaders are resourceful. They possess a creative mindset that allows them to think outside the box and explore unconventional approaches. When faced with unexpected obstacles, they do not get stuck in rigid thinking or rely solely on existing plans. Instead, they leverage their resourcefulness to find new strategies, tap into different resources, or seek innovative solutions.

Embracing adaptability also means being open to feedback and input from others. Adaptable leaders recognize that they do not have all the answers and that collaboration is essential in finding the best path forward. They actively seek diverse perspectives, encourage dialogue, and create an environment where team members feel comfortable sharing their ideas and concerns. By fostering a culture of collaboration, adaptable leaders tap into the collective intelligence and creativity of their teams, enhancing their ability to overcome challenges and find effective solutions.

Adaptable leaders are quick to recognize when a particular approach or strategy is not yielding the desired results. They are not wedded to their initial plans or ideas but are willing to pivot and make necessary changes. They possess the humility to acknowledge when adjustments are needed and the courage to make decisive shifts in direction. This flexibility allows them to adapt to new circumstances, seize emerging opportunities, and optimize outcomes.

Adaptable leaders also excel in managing change. They understand that change is constant and inevitable in today's dynamic and fast-paced world. Rather than resisting or fearing change, they embrace it as an opportunity for growth and progress. They proactively anticipate and prepare for change, communicate its significance to their teams, and provide the necessary support and resources to navigate through transitions successfully.

Leaders who embrace adaptability demonstrate resilience and resourcefulness. They view setbacks and unexpected obstacles as learning opportunities and leverage them to find alternative solutions. Their open-mindedness, resourcefulness, and willingness to embrace change enable them to navigate through challenges and lead their teams to success. By embodying adaptability, leaders foster a culture of innovation, creativity, and resilience, ultimately driving positive and sustainable outcomes for their organizations.

KEY TAKEAWAY

Agility is closely linked to adaptability, as it involves the ability to respond quickly and effectively to changing circumstances.

Leaders who dig the ditches are able to make timely decisions, mobilize resources, and adjust their strategies to stay aligned with their evolving expectations. They are willing to take calculated risks and experiment with new approaches, knowing that flexibility and agility are crucial in a rapidly changing world.

Leaders who embody adaptability and agility create a culture of innovation and learning within their teams. They encourage their team members to embrace change, experiment with new ideas, and constantly seek improvement. By fostering a culture of adaptability, leaders empower their teams to respond effectively to challenges, embrace change, and capitalize on emerging opportunities.

KEY TAKEAWAY

Leaders who expect around the reality understand the importance of adaptability and agility. They are able to adjust their expectations and plans in response to changing circumstances. By embodying adaptability and agility, leaders inspire their teams to embrace change, find creative solutions, and ultimately achieve extraordinary outcomes.

Summary

Leaders who expect around the reality that has their attention demonstrate the power of belief, vision, and proactive planning. By embracing this concept, leaders shape their reality, overcome obstacles, and inspire their teams to achieve extraordinary results. Through a combination of unwavering expectations, strategic planning, adaptability, and motivation, leaders dig the ditches and create pathways to success. By embodying this approach, leaders have the potential to transform their organizations and leave a lasting impact on those they lead.

Leadership
KEY C〇NCEPTS

14

Fall in Love With an Idea
Leaders Are Thankful and Grateful for the Idea that Used Them

Introduction

In the realm of leadership, there are instances when an idea captures the hearts and minds of individuals, propelling them to take action and make a significant impact. Great leaders not only embrace these ideas but also develop a deep sense of gratitude and appreciation for the opportunities that arise from them. We will explore the notion that leaders who fall in love with an idea are thankful and grateful for the idea that used them. By examining the qualities and behaviors associated with such leaders, we can gain insights into the transformative power of ideas and the profound gratitude that emerges from their pursuit.

1. The Power of Ideas

In the realm of leadership, ideas hold immense power. They have the potential to ignite passion, drive change, and shape the course of our world. When leaders encounter an idea that deeply resonates with them, it has the capacity to capture their imagination and propel them towards meaningful action. This paper explores the power of ideas and how they inspire, motivate, and drive change in the lives of leaders and those around them.

Inspiration: Ideas serve as a wellspring of inspiration for leaders. When they come across an idea that aligns with their values and vision, it sparks their imagination and stirs their passion. The idea becomes a source of inspiration, fueling their desire to make a difference and create a positive impact. It provides them with a sense of purpose and a clear direction for their leadership journey.

Motivation: Ideas possess the power to motivate leaders to take action. When leaders connect with an idea that resonates deeply with them, it becomes a driving force that propels them forward. The idea creates a sense of urgency and a strong inner drive to transform it into a reality. This motivation fuels their determination, resilience, and perseverance, enabling them to overcome obstacles and setbacks along the way.

Change Catalyst: Ideas are catalysts for change. They possess the potential to challenge the status quo, disrupt existing systems, and introduce innovative solutions. When leaders encounter an idea that holds transformative potential, they recognize the opportunity to bring about positive change. They become change agents, working tirelessly to translate the idea into actionable strategies and initiatives. By embracing the power of the idea, leaders inspire others to join them in their quest for change.

Impactful Leadership: Leaders who are driven by powerful ideas possess a unique ability to inspire and influence others. The passion and conviction they have for the idea radiate through their words and actions, attracting like-minded individuals who are eager to contribute and support the cause. These leaders are adept at articulating the vision and potential impact of the idea, galvanizing their team and stakeholders to rally behind it. They create a shared sense of purpose and mobilize others towards collective action.

Transformational Outcomes: The power of ideas lies in their potential to transform individuals, organizations, and communities. When leaders fully embrace an idea, they channel their energy and resources towards translating it into tangible outcomes. They leverage their leadership skills, collaborate with others, and make strategic decisions that align with the idea's purpose. The pursuit of the idea leads to innovation, growth, and positive change, benefiting not only the leader but also those who are impacted by their actions.

Ideas possess an extraordinary power to inspire, motivate, and drive change in the lives of leaders and the world around them. When leaders encounter an idea that deeply resonates with them, it ignites their passion and fuels their motivation. Ideas become catalysts for transformation, shaping the way leaders think, act, and lead. By embracing the power of ideas, leaders can bring about positive change and create a lasting impact on individuals, organizations, and society as a whole.

KEY TAKEAWAY

2. Embracing the Idea

When leaders encounter an idea that deeply resonates with them, they don't merely acknowledge it superficially; they wholeheartedly embrace it. They understand that embracing the idea requires a commitment of their time, energy, and resources. They invest themselves fully in understanding the purpose and potential of the idea.

To embrace the idea, leaders engage in thorough research and exploration. They delve into the intricacies of the concept, seeking to understand its underlying principles, context, and implications. They immerse themselves in relevant literature, studies, and resources to gain a comprehensive understanding of the idea's foundations.

Leaders who fall in love with an idea actively seek knowledge and insights from various sources. They engage in meaningful conversations and dialogues with experts, thought leaders, and others who share their enthusiasm for the idea. They listen intently, ask thoughtful questions, and absorb diverse perspectives. By actively engaging in dialogue, leaders expand their understanding of the idea and challenge their own assumptions.

Through this process of immersion and exploration, leaders gain a deep appreciation for the idea's purpose and potential. They develop a comprehensive understanding of how the idea can be applied and the impact it can have in their specific context. This knowledge equips them to make informed decisions and take deliberate action in pursuing the idea's realization.

Additionally, leaders who embrace an idea recognize that they do not possess all the answers. They are humble enough to seek guidance and input from others, recognizing the value of collaboration and shared learning. They actively seek out opportunities to engage with individuals who may have different perspectives or expertise related to the idea. This open-mindedness allows leaders to refine their understanding and incorporate valuable insights into their approach.

KEY TAKEAWAY

By embracing the idea wholeheartedly, leaders demonstrate a commitment to its purpose and potential. They invest their time, energy, and resources to deeply understand the idea and its implications. Through research, dialogue, and collaboration, they gain a comprehensive understanding of the idea's intricacies and broaden their perspective. This commitment and knowledge enable leaders to make informed decisions and take purposeful action in bringing the idea to life.

3. Gratitude and Thankfulness

Leaders who fall in love with an idea not only embrace it with passion and commitment, but they also develop a profound sense of gratitude and thankfulness. They recognize that the idea has chosen them as instruments for its manifestation and impact. This recognition instills a deep appreciation for the opportunity to be part of something greater than themselves.

Gratitude and thankfulness arise from a genuine understanding of the significance and potential of the idea. Leaders realize that they have been entrusted with a unique opportunity to contribute to a greater purpose. They acknowledge that their connection with the idea is not merely a coincidence but a meaningful alignment of their values, passions, and capabilities.

The gratitude leaders feel stems from the realization that they have the chance to make a difference. They understand that the idea has the potential to positively impact individuals, communities, or even the world at large. This awareness fuels their commitment and dedication to bringing the idea to fruition, as they recognize the responsibility and privilege of being part of such a transformative journey.

Gratitude also fosters a sense of humility within leaders. They acknowledge that they are not solely responsible for the idea's success, but rather part of a larger network of individuals, circumstances, and opportunities that have converged to make the idea possible. They appreciate the contributions and support of others who have influenced their path and provided resources, guidance, or inspiration along the way.

Leaders who cultivate gratitude and thankfulness understand that their connection to the idea is reciprocal. They realize that the idea enriches their lives, providing them with purpose, meaning, and fulfillment. The gratitude they feel is an acknowledgment of the personal growth, learning, and transformation that they experience as they engage with the idea. They are grateful for the ways in which the idea has challenged and stretched them, ultimately making them better leaders and individuals.

Leaders who express gratitude and thankfulness for the idea they have fallen in love with demonstrate a deep respect and reverence for the opportunity they have been given. This gratitude serves as a driving force, fueling their commitment, resilience, and perseverance in the face of challenges. It also allows them to approach their leadership journey with a sense of joy, appreciation, and humility.

> *Leaders who fall in love with an idea develop a profound sense of gratitude and thankfulness. They recognize the significance of being chosen as vehicles for the idea's manifestation and impact. This gratitude fuels their commitment, dedication, and humility, as they appreciate the opportunity to contribute to a greater purpose. By embracing gratitude, leaders foster a deeper connection with the idea, infusing their leadership journey with purpose, fulfillment, and a genuine appreciation for the transformative power of their chosen path.*

KEY TAKEAWAY

4. Inspiration and Motivation

Leaders who fall in love with an idea become deeply inspired and motivated by its potential. The idea serves as a catalyst, igniting their passion and driving them forward with unwavering determination. It becomes a source of energy, resilience, and unwavering commitment.

The inspiration that leaders derive from the idea is transformative. It sparks their imagination, ignites their creativity, and propels them to think beyond existing boundaries and limitations. The idea captivates their thoughts, filling them with a sense of purpose and direction. They envision the positive impact that the idea can have on individuals, organizations, or society as a whole, and this vision fuels their inspiration.

This inspiration goes beyond mere enthusiasm; it becomes a driving force that compels leaders to take action. It motivates them to step out of their comfort zones, embrace challenges, and persevere in the face of obstacles. Even when confronted with setbacks or failures, the inspiration derived from the idea provides leaders with the resilience to bounce back, learn from their experiences, and continue moving forward.

Leaders who are inspired by an idea also inspire others. Their passion and unwavering belief in the idea are contagious, rallying others around the cause. They communicate the vision and potential impact of the idea with clarity and enthusiasm, motivating their team members and stakeholders to join their efforts. Through their inspired leadership, they create a shared sense of purpose and a collective drive to bring the idea to fruition.

The motivation that leaders derive from the idea is a powerful force that propels them forward. It instills in them a deep sense of commitment and dedication. The idea becomes a personal mission, and leaders are driven to see it through, no matter the obstacles they encounter along the way.

The motivation derived from the idea allows leaders to maintain focus, even in the face of distractions or competing priorities. It helps them prioritize their actions, make strategic decisions, and allocate resources effectively. The idea serves as a compass, guiding their leadership journey and ensuring that their efforts remain aligned with their ultimate goal.

Leaders who are inspired and motivated by an idea are more likely to inspire and motivate others. Their passion, dedication, and unwavering belief in the idea create a positive and energizing environment. They inspire their team members to embrace the idea, invest their own enthusiasm and energy, and strive for excellence in their work.

5. Honoring the Idea

Leaders who are grateful for the idea that has chosen them understand the importance of honoring it. They recognize that the idea carries a purpose and set of values that must be respected and upheld. To honor the idea, leaders align their actions, decisions, and behaviors with its essence.

Alignment with the purpose and values of the idea requires leaders to deeply understand and internalize them. They take the time to reflect on the core principles and objectives behind the idea, ensuring that their actions are in harmony with its intended direction. By doing so, leaders ensure that they are moving in sync with the idea's vision and mission.

Respect is a fundamental aspect of honoring the idea. Leaders approach their work with humility and an appreciation for the idea's significance. They acknowledge that they are merely stewards of the idea, entrusted with the responsibility of bringing it to life. This recognition instills a sense of reverence, prompting leaders to treat the idea with the utmost respect and care.

Integrity is another key element of honoring the idea. Leaders who are grateful for the idea ensure that their actions are aligned with their values and the values inherent in the idea. They consistently act in accordance with ethical standards, making decisions that reflect honesty, transparency, and fairness. By demonstrating integrity, leaders build trust, not only with their team members but also with stakeholders and others who are involved in the realization of the idea.

Leaders approach their work with a deep sense of responsibility. They understand that their actions and behaviors reflect not only on themselves but also on the idea they have embraced. They recognize that their leadership serves as a representation of the idea, and they hold themselves accountable for upholding its values and integrity. This responsibility drives leaders to strive for excellence, continuously seeking ways to improve their skills, knowledge, and effectiveness as they work towards manifesting the idea.

By honoring the idea, leaders create a positive and authentic connection with it. Their actions and behaviors align with the purpose and values of the idea, ensuring that they are in complete harmony with its essence. This alignment allows leaders to be effective ambassadors for the idea, inspiring others through their integrity, dedication, and commitment. It also fosters a sense of trust and authenticity within their teams and stakeholders, creating an environment conducive to collaboration and shared success.

KEY TAKEAWAY

Leaders who are grateful for the idea they have fallen in love with honor it by aligning their actions with its purpose and values. They approach their work with respect, integrity, and a deep sense of responsibility. By doing so, they uphold the essence of the idea and ensure that their leadership is a true reflection of its vision and mission. Through their dedication and commitment, these leaders create an environment where the idea can thrive, bringing about positive change and impact.

6. Creating Impact

Leaders who fall in love with an idea and express gratitude for it are driven by a deep desire to create meaningful impact. They understand that the idea has the potential to bring about positive change and improve the lives of individuals, organizations, or society as a whole. With their commitment and dedication, they channel their passion, skills, and resources towards transforming the idea into a tangible reality.

One of the ways leaders create impact is by aligning their actions with the purpose and values of the idea. They ensure that every decision, strategy, and initiative they undertake is guided by the idea's intended impact. By maintaining this alignment, leaders create a clear and focused path towards achieving the desired outcomes.

Leaders who are grateful for the idea also understand the importance of inspiring and empowering others to join their cause. They recognize that creating lasting impact requires the collective effort of a motivated and engaged team. These leaders communicate the vision, purpose, and potential impact of the idea in a compelling and inspiring manner. They share their passion, demonstrating how the idea can make a difference and inviting others to be part of the journey.

Through their leadership, these grateful leaders empower individuals within their teams. They provide support, guidance, and resources, enabling others to contribute their unique skills and perspectives. By fostering a sense of ownership and shared responsibility, leaders multiply their impact by tapping into the collective intelligence and capabilities of their team members.

Leaders who are committed to creating impact foster an environment that encourages innovation and creativity. They recognize that meaningful change often requires thinking beyond traditional approaches and finding novel solutions. These leaders create a culture that values experimentation, risk-taking, and learning from failures. By fostering an atmosphere of trust and psychological safety, they inspire their teams to think creatively and explore new possibilities.

In addition to inspiring and empowering their teams, grateful leaders also engage stakeholders and build strategic partnerships. They recognize the importance of collaborating with individuals and organizations who share a common vision and can contribute complementary expertise or resources. By cultivating these partnerships, leaders leverage collective strength and expertise, amplifying the impact of their efforts.

Creating impact is not a one-time accomplishment; it requires ongoing assessment, reflection, and adaptation. Leaders who are grateful for the idea understand the importance of monitoring progress and measuring outcomes. They use data and feedback to evaluate the effectiveness of their strategies and make necessary adjustments to optimize impact. This continuous improvement mindset allows them to adapt their approach and ensure that their efforts are making a meaningful difference.

KEY TAKEAWAY

Leaders who embrace an idea with gratitude and thankfulness are committed to creating meaningful impact. They channel their passion, skills, and resources towards transforming the idea into a reality that brings about positive change. Through inspiring and empowering others, fostering a culture of innovation, building strategic partnerships, and embracing a continuous improvement mindset, these leaders multiply their impact and create a ripple effect of positive change. By their dedication and commitment, they leave a lasting legacy of meaningful impact in the world.

Summary

Leaders who fall in love with an idea are thankful and grateful for the idea that used them. They recognize the transformative power of ideas and appreciate the opportunities they bring. With gratitude and thankfulness, these leaders embrace the idea, derive inspiration and motivation from it, and honor it through their actions. Their commitment to creating impact drives them to persevere and overcome obstacles along the way. By understanding the profound gratitude that emerges from the pursuit of an idea, we gain insights into the transformative potential of ideas and the qualities that make great leaders.

Leadership
KEY C●NCEPTS

15

Those Who Focus Always Thrive
Leaders Give Themselves a Command and Follow It

Introduction

In the realm of leadership, focus is a powerful attribute that distinguishes exceptional leaders from the rest. Leaders who possess unwavering focus give themselves a command—a clear direction—and then diligently follow it. We will explore the significance of focus in leadership and how leaders who prioritize it can thrive in their endeavors. By examining the qualities and behaviors associated with focused leadership, we gain insights into the transformative power of staying committed to a chosen path.

1. The Power of Focus

In the realm of leadership, focus is a crucial element that sets exceptional leaders apart. Leaders who possess the power of focus are able to direct their attention, energy, and efforts towards specific goals and tasks. By avoiding distractions and honing in on what truly matters, these leaders enhance their effectiveness, efficiency, and productivity. This paper explores the significance of focus in leadership and how it contributes to achieving greater success.

Clarity and Purpose: Focus begins with clarity of purpose. Leaders who are focused have a clear understanding of their goals and objectives. They know what they want to achieve and why it is important. This clarity provides a solid foundation for their focus, enabling them to prioritize their actions and make decisions that align with their overarching vision.

Eliminating Distractions: One of the key aspects of focus is the ability to eliminate distractions. Leaders who are focused are adept at recognizing and minimizing distractions that can divert their attention and hinder progress. They understand the importance of creating an environment that supports their focus by eliminating unnecessary noise, interruptions, and time-wasting activities. By eliminating distractions, leaders can maintain a laser-like focus on the tasks at hand.

Effective Time Management: Leaders who possess the power of focus are skilled in managing their time effectively. They prioritize their tasks and allocate dedicated time blocks to focus on specific activities. They understand that time is a finite resource and that every minute counts. By managing their time effectively, focused leaders maximize their productivity and make the most of their available resources.

Enhanced Decision-making: Focus plays a critical role in decision-making. Leaders who are focused are able to filter out irrelevant information and focus on the key factors that impact their decisions. They avoid decision paralysis by quickly assessing the relevant information and making informed choices aligned with their goals and values. By having a clear focus, leaders can make timely and effective decisions, driving their teams and organizations forward.

Increased Productivity: Focused leaders are highly productive. They are able to channel their energy and efforts towards tasks that align with their goals, avoiding unproductive or low-value activities. By concentrating their resources on the most important priorities, they are able to achieve more in less time. Focused leaders also possess the ability to stay on track, even when faced with challenges or setbacks, enabling them to maintain a consistent level of productivity.

Achievement of Goals: The power of focus lies in its ability to help leaders achieve their goals. By concentrating their efforts on what truly matters, leaders can make significant progress towards their desired outcomes. Focused leaders set specific and measurable goals, break them down into actionable steps, and consistently work towards their achievement. This level of focus and dedication increases the likelihood of success and allows leaders to make a tangible impact.

Focus is a fundamental attribute of effective leadership. Leaders who possess the power of focus are able to direct their attention, energy, and efforts towards specific goals and tasks. By eliminating distractions, managing their time effectively, making informed decisions, and enhancing productivity, these leaders achieve greater success. The power of focus lies in its ability to enhance effectiveness, efficiency, and productivity, enabling leaders to make a significant impact in their endeavors. By harnessing the power of focus, leaders can unlock their full potential and drive their teams and organizations towards success.

KEY TAKEAWAY

2. Clarity of Purpose

Clarity of purpose is a defining characteristic of leaders who give themselves a command and wholeheartedly follow it. These leaders possess a deep understanding of their goals, objectives, and desired outcomes. They have taken the time to reflect on their vision and values, allowing them to establish a clear sense of purpose that guides their actions and decisions.

Leaders with a clear sense of purpose understand the "why" behind their goals. They have a profound understanding of the impact they want to make and the difference they aim to create. This clarity empowers them to set meaningful priorities and make informed decisions that align with their overarching vision. Every action they take is driven by their purpose, ensuring that their efforts are purposeful and intentional.

By focusing on their purpose, leaders create a sense of direction not only for themselves but also for those around them. They inspire and motivate others by communicating their vision and the underlying purpose behind it. Their clarity of purpose serves as a beacon, guiding their team members and stakeholders towards shared goals and objectives. This sense of direction fosters alignment, collaboration, and a shared sense of meaning and fulfillment within the organization.

Leaders who possess clarity of purpose are more resilient and adaptable in the face of challenges and uncertainties. They understand that setbacks and obstacles are inevitable on the path to achieving their goals. However, their clear sense of purpose provides them with a solid foundation and the determination to persevere. They are able to navigate through difficult times with conviction and resilience, staying focused on their purpose even in the midst of adversity.

Leaders who are guided by a clear purpose are more effective in decision-making. When faced with choices and dilemmas, they can evaluate options against their purpose, values, and long-term goals. This clarity enables them to make decisions that align with their vision and values, leading to more meaningful and sustainable outcomes.

Clarity of purpose also brings a sense of authenticity and credibility to leaders. When leaders are clear about their purpose, they exude confidence and conviction. Their words and actions are aligned with their vision, and they inspire trust and confidence in others. This authenticity attracts followers and garners support from team members, stakeholders, and other leaders who resonate with their purpose.

KEY TAKEAWAY

Leaders who give themselves a command and follow it possess a clear sense of purpose. They understand their goals, objectives, and desired outcomes at a deep level. This clarity allows them to set meaningful priorities, make informed decisions, and inspire others to follow suit. By focusing on their purpose, these leaders create a sense of direction, foster alignment, and navigate challenges with resilience. Clarity of purpose serves as a guiding force, empowering leaders to make a positive and lasting impact on individuals, organizations, and society as a whole.

3. Setting Priorities

Setting priorities is a vital aspect of focused leadership. Leaders who understand the significance of prioritization are able to distinguish between urgent and important tasks. They recognize that not all tasks hold the same level of significance or contribute equally to their goals. By effectively prioritizing their time and resources, focused leaders ensure that their attention and efforts are directed towards activities that have the greatest impact on their objectives.

Effective prioritization begins with a clear understanding of the goals and desired outcomes. Focused leaders take the time to identify and define their priorities, aligning them with their overarching vision and purpose. They assess the importance and urgency of each task or responsibility, considering factors such as the potential impact on their goals, timelines, and available resources.

By prioritizing effectively, leaders ensure that they invest their time and resources where they will yield the greatest returns. They allocate their energy towards tasks and initiatives that directly contribute to their desired outcomes. This strategic approach allows leaders to focus on activities that align with their strengths, expertise, and core competencies, maximizing their productivity and impact.

Effective prioritization enables leaders to manage their time and resources efficiently. They understand that time is a valuable resource and that it must be allocated judiciously to achieve optimal results. Focused leaders make conscious choices about how to spend their time, ensuring that they dedicate sufficient attention to high-priority tasks while minimizing or delegating lower-priority responsibilities.

In addition to allocating time, focused leaders also allocate resources based on their priorities. They ensure that resources such as budget, manpower, and technology are allocated to initiatives that align with their strategic objectives. By directing resources towards high-priority projects, leaders optimize their potential for success and ensure that resources are utilized effectively.

Setting priorities also involves the ability to make tough decisions and say no to non-essential or low-value tasks. Focused leaders understand that not every opportunity or request aligns with their priorities. They have the courage to decline or delegate tasks that do not contribute significantly to their goals. This discipline allows leaders to maintain focus on what truly matters and avoid spreading themselves too thin.

By effectively setting priorities, focused leaders are able to maintain clarity and direction amidst a multitude of responsibilities and distractions. They can better manage their time, energy, and resources, ensuring that they are channeled towards activities that have the greatest impact on their objectives. This strategic approach enhances their productivity, efficiency, and overall effectiveness as leaders.

Setting priorities is a crucial aspect of focused leadership. Leaders who prioritize effectively are able to distinguish between urgent and important tasks, allocating their time and resources accordingly. By focusing on activities that have the greatest impact on their goals, leaders maximize their productivity and achieve optimal results. Effective prioritization enables leaders to make conscious choices, manage their time and resources efficiently, and maintain clarity and direction amidst competing demands. By setting priorities, focused leaders position themselves for success and ensure that their efforts are aligned with their desired outcomes.

4. Resilience and Perseverance

Resilience and perseverance are inherent qualities of focused leaders. These leaders understand that challenges and setbacks are an inevitable part of the journey towards achieving their goals. Instead of being discouraged or deterred by obstacles, they view them as opportunities for growth and learning.

Focused leaders possess a mindset that embraces resilience. They are not easily shaken by adversity or unexpected hurdles. Instead, they remain steadfast in their commitment to their chosen path and maintain a positive outlook. They understand that setbacks are temporary and that perseverance is key to overcoming them.

In the face of challenges, focused leaders adapt and innovate. They remain open-minded and flexible, seeking alternative solutions and approaches. They leverage their creativity and problem-solving skills to find new ways to navigate obstacles and continue progressing towards their goals. They understand that rigid adherence to a specific plan may not always be effective, and they are willing to adjust their strategies when necessary.

Focused leaders possess the ability to learn from their experiences. They reflect on the challenges they encounter and extract valuable lessons and insights. They see setbacks as opportunities for personal and professional growth, using them as stepping stones to enhance their knowledge, skills, and resilience. This continuous learning mindset allows them to develop greater adaptability and fortitude in the face of future challenges.

Focused leaders surround themselves with a supportive network. They seek guidance and support from mentors, advisors, and peers who can provide guidance and encouragement during difficult times. They understand the importance of leaning on others for support and drawing strength from collective wisdom. This support system helps them maintain their focus and remain motivated when faced with adversity.

Focused leaders also possess a strong sense of purpose and passion. Their unwavering focus stems from their deep commitment to their goals and their belief in the value of their chosen path. This passion fuels their perseverance, enabling them to push through challenges and setbacks. They are driven by a desire to make a difference and are willing to put in the necessary effort and endurance to achieve their vision.

Resilience and perseverance are integral qualities of focused leaders. These leaders understand that challenges and setbacks are part of the journey towards success. They view obstacles as opportunities for growth and learning, adapt and innovate in the face of adversity, and maintain an unwavering focus on their goals. Through their resilience and perseverance, focused leaders navigate challenges with determination and emerge stronger and more capable. Their ability to overcome obstacles inspires their teams and stakeholders and positions them for long-term success.

KEY TAKEAWAY

5. Eliminating Distractions

Eliminating distractions is a crucial aspect of focused leadership. Leaders who are able to actively minimize and manage distractions are better equipped to dedicate their attention and resources to their command, maximizing their potential for success. These leaders cultivate discipline and develop strategies to maintain focus amidst various internal and external interruptions.

One of the key strategies employed by focused leaders is setting clear boundaries. They establish boundaries to protect their time, energy, and attention. This may involve establishing designated periods of uninterrupted work or creating dedicated spaces for focused activities. By defining boundaries, leaders create an environment that minimizes distractions and promotes deep focus on their command.

Time management techniques are another effective tool utilized by focused leaders to eliminate distractions. They prioritize their tasks and allocate specific time blocks to work on critical activities. They may use techniques such as the Pomodoro Technique, time blocking, or implementing productivity apps and tools to enhance their efficiency and protect themselves from time-wasting distractions.

In addition to external distractions, focused leaders also recognize the importance of managing internal distractions. They cultivate self-discipline by developing practices that help them maintain focus. This may involve techniques such as mindfulness exercises, meditation, or self-reflection to quiet the mind and reduce internal distractions. They also practice self-awareness, identifying their own tendencies and triggers for distraction and proactively addressing them.

Focused leaders understand the value of creating a conducive work environment. They minimize distractions by organizing their physical space, removing clutter, and creating a dedicated space that promotes concentration. They may establish protocols or guidelines for communication within their team or organization to minimize interruptions and unnecessary distractions.

Focused leaders exhibit the ability to prioritize effectively. They recognize that not all tasks and requests are equally important or aligned with their command. They have the discipline to say no to non-essential or low-value activities that could divert their attention from their primary goals. By selectively choosing where to invest their time and energy, focused leaders ensure that they can fully dedicate themselves to activities that align with their command and have the greatest impact.

By actively eliminating distractions, focused leaders create an environment that supports deep focus and concentration. They are able to allocate their attention and resources to their command, enabling them to achieve higher levels of productivity and effectiveness. Their ability to minimize distractions allows them to maintain clarity, make informed decisions, and work towards their goals with unwavering focus.

Leaders who actively minimize and manage distractions cultivate discipline, establish boundaries, and implement strategies to maintain focus. By protecting their time, energy, and attention from distractions, these leaders maximize their potential for success. They create an environment that fosters deep concentration and allows them to fully dedicate themselves to their command, resulting in higher levels of productivity and achievement.

KEY TAKEAWAY

6. Building a Supportive Environment

Building a supportive environment is a key aspect of focused leadership. Leaders who prioritize focus understand that it is not an individual endeavor but a collective effort. They create a culture that supports and encourages focus by fostering clarity, discipline, and accountability within their teams or organizations.

One way focused leaders build a supportive environment is by clearly communicating expectations. They provide a clear vision and purpose to their team members, ensuring that everyone understands the shared command and the importance of staying focused on it. By articulating expectations, leaders create a common understanding and a sense of direction that guides the efforts of the entire team.

Focused leaders provide the necessary resources for their team members to maintain focus. They ensure that their teams have access to the tools, technologies, and information needed to effectively carry out their tasks. By eliminating barriers and providing the necessary resources, leaders empower their team members to focus on their responsibilities and contribute to the shared command.

In addition to communication and resource provision, focused leaders foster discipline within their teams. They set an example by maintaining their own discipline and demonstrating their commitment to the shared command. They establish routines, processes, and systems that support focus and minimize distractions. By promoting discipline, leaders create an environment where individuals are encouraged to maintain their focus and stay committed to the shared goals.

Accountability is a fundamental element of a supportive environment for focused leaders. They establish mechanisms to hold themselves and their team members accountable for staying focused on the command. This may involve regular check-ins, progress tracking, or performance evaluations. By creating a culture of accountability, leaders ensure that focus remains a priority and that everyone is aligned with the shared command.

Focused leaders also empower their team members to align their efforts and achieve collective goals. They foster collaboration and teamwork, encouraging individuals to support and motivate one another in maintaining focus. They create opportunities for open communication, sharing progress, and celebrating milestones. By fostering a sense of collective ownership and shared responsibility, leaders create an environment where focus is valued and reinforced by the entire team.

By building a supportive environment that encourages focus, leaders enable their teams to work together towards the shared command. They create a culture where clarity, discipline, and accountability thrive. In such an environment, individuals are empowered to stay focused on their responsibilities, contribute to the collective goals, and overcome distractions and obstacles together.

KEY TAKEAWAY

Building a supportive environment is a crucial aspect of focused leadership. Leaders who prioritize focus foster a culture of clarity, discipline, and accountability. By communicating expectations, providing necessary resources, promoting discipline, and encouraging accountability, leaders create an environment where focus is valued and supported. In such an environment, team members are empowered to align their efforts, achieve collective goals, and overcome challenges to make progress towards the shared command.

Summary

Leaders who give themselves a command and follow it with unwavering focus possess a powerful advantage in achieving their desired outcomes. Through clarity of purpose, effective prioritization, resilience, elimination of distractions, and fostering a supportive environment, focused leaders maximize their potential for success. Their ability to maintain focus enables them to navigate challenges, stay committed to their chosen path, and inspire others to do the same. By their unwavering commitment and dedication, focused leaders thrive in their endeavors, leaving a lasting impact on individuals, organizations, and society as a whole.

Leadership
KEY C🔑NCEPTS

16

We Get What We Give
Leaders Cannot Escape the Results of Their Beliefs

Introduction

Leadership is not just about actions and decisions; it is deeply rooted in the beliefs and convictions of those who lead. The beliefs held by leaders shape their perspectives, guide their decision-making, and ultimately influence the outcomes they achieve. We will explore the idea that leaders cannot escape the results of their beliefs. By examining the impact of beliefs on leadership effectiveness, we gain insights into the profound influence of belief systems in shaping the outcomes leaders achieve.

The Power of Beliefs

Beliefs play a significant role in shaping a leader's mindset, perspectives, and ultimately their actions and outcomes. They serve as the foundation upon which a leader's worldview is built, influencing how they perceive themselves, others, and the world. This paper explores the power of beliefs in leadership and how they impact a leader's thoughts, emotions, behaviors, and ultimately the results they achieve.

Shaping Mindset and Perspective: Beliefs act as the lens through which leaders view the world. They shape their mindset and determine how they interpret and respond to situations.

Positive beliefs, such as believing in one's own capabilities and the potential for growth, foster a growth mindset. This mindset empowers leaders to embrace challenges, persist in the face of setbacks, and see opportunities for learning and improvement. On the other hand, negative beliefs, such as self-doubt or fixed mindsets, can hinder a leader's confidence, resilience, and ability to adapt.

Influencing Thoughts and Emotions: Beliefs have a profound impact on a leader's thoughts and emotions. What leaders believe about themselves, their team, and their organization affects their self-talk, self-perception, and emotional state. Beliefs that instill confidence, optimism, and a sense of purpose can fuel motivation, enthusiasm, and a positive emotional state. Conversely, limiting beliefs or negative self-perceptions can lead to self-sabotaging thoughts, self-doubt, and negative emotions that hinder performance and decision-making.

Guiding Behavior and Actions: Beliefs strongly influence a leader's behavior and actions. Leaders who hold beliefs aligned with their goals, values, and vision are more likely to take consistent and purposeful actions. These beliefs provide a guidepost for decision-making and help leaders stay focused on their desired outcomes. Leaders with a strong belief in their team members' capabilities are more likely to delegate authority, empower their team, and foster collaboration. Their beliefs in their own abilities and the potential for success drive them to take risks, persevere, and make bold decisions.

Impacting Organizational Culture: Beliefs held by leaders shape the culture within an organization. A leader's beliefs about trust, transparency, accountability, and collaboration directly influence the values and norms that permeate the organization. If a leader believes in open communication, fairness, and inclusivity, they will foster a culture that promotes these principles. On the contrary, if a leader holds beliefs rooted in hierarchy, control, or competition, the resulting culture may inhibit collaboration, stifle creativity, and foster a sense of disengagement.

Creating a Positive Work Environment: Leaders' beliefs have a direct impact on the work environment they create. Beliefs about the value and potential of their team members influence the way leaders interact, motivate, and support their teams. When leaders hold positive beliefs about their team's abilities, they create an environment that promotes growth, trust, and empowerment. This positive work environment fosters engagement, creativity, and high performance. In contrast, leaders with limiting beliefs may unintentionally undermine their team's potential, leading to low morale, disengagement, and reduced productivity.

Challenging and Evolving Beliefs: Leadership growth involves challenging and evolving one's beliefs. Effective leaders recognize that beliefs are not fixed, and they actively seek opportunities to expand their belief systems. They remain open-minded, seek diverse perspectives, and engage in continuous learning. By challenging and evolving their beliefs, leaders gain new insights, embrace innovation, and adapt their strategies to achieve better results.

> *Beliefs form the bedrock of a leader's mindset, perspectives, and actions. They shape a leader's thoughts, emotions, behaviors, and ultimately the results they achieve. Positive beliefs foster a growth mindset, empowering leaders to embrace challenges, persist in the face of adversity, and achieve greater success. Leaders who consciously cultivate empowering beliefs create a positive work environment, foster engagement, and inspire their teams to reach their full potential. By recognizing the power of beliefs and continually evolving them, leaders can unlock their true potential and drive positive outcomes in their personal and professional lives.*

KEY
TAKEAWAY

2. Self-Fulfilling Prophecy

The self-fulfilling prophecy effect is a powerful phenomenon that highlights the impact of leaders' beliefs on their outcomes. Leaders who hold positive beliefs about their abilities, the potential for growth, and the capacity for success often experience a self-fulfilling prophecy effect, leading to higher levels of achievement.

When leaders believe in their abilities and have confidence in their skills, they approach challenges with a positive mindset. They view obstacles as opportunities for growth and learning rather than insurmountable barriers. This optimistic outlook drives proactive behaviors, as they actively seek solutions, take calculated risks, and persist in the face of setbacks. Their belief in their own capabilities fuels their motivation and determination to overcome challenges and achieve success.

Leaders who hold positive beliefs are more likely to inspire and motivate others. Their confidence and belief in their team's potential create an environment of trust and empowerment. They encourage their team members to embrace challenges, develop their skills, and strive for excellence. This positive influence cascades throughout the team, fostering a culture of growth and achievement.

Conversely, leaders who hold negative beliefs may experience a self-fulfilling prophecy effect that limits their potential. If a leader doubts their abilities or fears failure, they may be reluctant to take risks or seize opportunities. This mindset can create a cycle of self-doubt and fear that hinders their progress. Their negative beliefs may also affect their team, leading to a lack of confidence, disengagement, and reduced performance.

It is important for leaders to recognize the power of their beliefs and the impact they have on their outcomes. By cultivating positive beliefs, leaders can enhance their self-confidence, resilience, and willingness to take risks. They can actively challenge negative beliefs and replace them with empowering ones that support their growth and success.

Developing a positive belief system requires self-reflection, self-awareness, and intentional mindset shifts. Leaders can engage in practices such as positive affirmations, visualization, and cognitive reframing to foster positive beliefs. They can seek feedback and surround themselves with supportive individuals who reinforce their positive beliefs and challenge any self-limiting beliefs.

KEY TAKEAWAY

Leaders' beliefs have a self-fulfilling prophecy effect on their outcomes. Positive beliefs about their abilities, growth potential, and success can lead to proactive behaviors, increased motivation, and ultimately higher levels of achievement. Conversely, negative beliefs can limit a leader's potential, resulting in self-doubt, fear, and a reluctance to take risks. Leaders must cultivate positive beliefs, challenge negative ones, and foster a growth mindset to unlock their full potential and drive success for themselves and their teams.

3. Influence on Decision-making

Beliefs play a significant role in shaping leaders' decision-making processes. The beliefs they hold about themselves, their team members, and the organization strongly influence their perceptions, biases, and preferences. These beliefs act as filters through which leaders interpret information, assess situations, and make choices.

When leaders hold positive beliefs about the potential and capabilities of their team members, they are more likely to delegate authority and empower their team. They trust their team members' abilities to contribute meaningfully and make decisions. This belief in their team's capabilities fosters an environment of collaboration, where team members are encouraged to share their ideas, take initiative, and assume ownership of their work. By delegating authority, leaders allow their team members to grow, learn, and develop new skills, ultimately contributing to their personal and professional growth.

Leaders who hold positive beliefs about their team members create an environment of trust and empowerment. They believe in the competency and integrity of their team, which enables them to provide autonomy and support. This trust fosters a sense of ownership and accountability among team members, as they feel valued and empowered to make decisions aligned with the organization's goals. In such an environment, team members are more likely to take risks, contribute innovative ideas, and collaborate effectively, leading to enhanced creativity, productivity, and overall team performance.

On the other hand, leaders who hold limiting beliefs about their team's abilities may tend to micromanage and stifle creativity. These leaders may lack trust in their team members' capabilities and feel the need to closely oversee and control their work. Micromanagement not only hampers team members' autonomy and growth but also undermines their confidence and motivation. When leaders limit their team's decision-making authority, it stifles creativity, diminishes ownership, and inhibits the exploration of new ideas and approaches.

A leaders' belief about the organization itself can also influence their decision-making. If leaders have a positive belief in the organization's mission, values, and potential for success, they are more likely to make decisions that align with these beliefs. They may be willing to take calculated risks, invest in innovation, and pursue growth opportunities. Conversely, leaders who hold limiting beliefs about the organization's capabilities or future prospects may make conservative decisions that hinder progress or limit the organization's potential for growth.

Recognizing the influence of beliefs on decision-making is crucial for leaders. By cultivating positive beliefs about their team members' abilities, leaders can empower their team and foster a culture of trust and collaboration. Leaders can challenge any limiting beliefs they may hold and adopt a growth mindset that encourages innovation, risk-taking, and continuous improvement. Moreover, leaders should also evaluate their beliefs about the organization itself and ensure that their decisions align with a positive vision for the future.

KEY TAKEAWAY

Beliefs strongly influence leaders' decision-making processes. Positive beliefs about team members' potential and capabilities foster empowerment, collaboration, and trust. These beliefs enable leaders to delegate authority and create an environment that promotes growth and development. Conversely, limiting beliefs may lead to micromanagement, stifled creativity, and restricted decision-making authority. Leaders must recognize the influence of their beliefs and actively cultivate positive beliefs that align with their team's potential and the organization's goals.

4. Impact on Organizational Culture

The impact of leaders' beliefs on organizational culture cannot be overstated. The beliefs leaders hold shape the values, norms, and behaviors that are fostered and encouraged within the organization. These beliefs serve as guiding principles that influence how leaders interact with their teams, make decisions, and set expectations. As a result, the organizational culture reflects the beliefs and values upheld by its leaders.

Leaders who believe in transparency, open communication, and collaboration foster a culture that values these principles. They create an environment where information flows freely, ideas are shared, and diverse perspectives are encouraged. Such leaders promote a culture of trust, where employees feel comfortable speaking up, providing feedback, and engaging in open dialogue. In turn, this culture promotes innovation, creativity, and effective problem-solving, as individuals are encouraged to share their thoughts and work collaboratively towards shared goals.

On the other hand, leaders who hold beliefs rooted in hierarchy, control, and competition may create an environment characterized by silos, mistrust, and a lack of collaboration. When leaders prioritize control and maintain a hierarchical structure, communication channels become limited, and decision-making authority is concentrated at the top. This can hinder information sharing, stifle creativity, and create barriers between different teams or departments. Competition may prevail over collaboration, as individuals focus on outperforming each other rather than working together towards common objectives.

The beliefs leaders hold also influence how they set expectations and reward behaviors within the organization. Leaders who believe in inclusivity, respect, and fairness create a culture that values these principles. They set expectations for respectful communication, equal opportunities, and diversity. They reward behaviors that reflect these values, fostering an inclusive and supportive environment where everyone feels valued and respected.

Conversely, leaders who hold beliefs that prioritize individual achievement, hierarchy, or favoritism may create a culture where unfairness and inequality prevail. In such environments, employees may feel discouraged, disengaged, and unmotivated, as their efforts may not be recognized or rewarded based on merit.

To shape a positive organizational culture, leaders need to be aware of their beliefs and values and assess their impact on the organization. They should strive to align their beliefs with principles such as transparency, open communication, collaboration, inclusivity, and fairness. By leading by example and reinforcing these beliefs through their actions and decisions, leaders can create a culture that encourages positive behaviors and supports the organization's mission and goals.

Leaders' beliefs significantly influence the organizational culture. The beliefs leaders hold shape the values, norms, and behaviors that are encouraged and rewarded within the organization. Leaders who believe in transparency, open communication, and collaboration foster a culture that values these principles, promoting trust and innovation. Conversely, leaders with beliefs rooted in hierarchy, control, and competition may create a culture characterized by silos and lack of collaboration. To shape a positive organizational culture, leaders should be aware of their beliefs, align them with positive principles, and lead by example to create an environment that supports the organization's mission and values.

KEY TAKEAWAY

5. Influence on Employee Engagement

Leaders' beliefs have a profound impact on employee engagement within an organization. The beliefs leaders hold about their employees directly influence how they interact with and perceive their team members, which, in turn, shapes the level of engagement and motivation among employees.

When leaders believe in the value and importance of their employees, they create an environment that fosters engagement. Leaders who hold positive beliefs about their employees' capabilities and potential recognize the strengths and unique contributions of each individual. They see their employees as valuable assets to the organization and understand that their skills and talents can drive success. This belief in their employees' abilities motivates leaders to provide opportunities for growth, development, and meaningful work. By empowering their employees and leveraging their strengths, leaders create an environment where employees feel valued, appreciated, and motivated to give their best.

Leaders who believe in their employees' potential provide opportunities for growth and development. They understand that investing in their employees' professional growth not only benefits individuals but also contributes to the overall success of the organization. Leaders with this belief provide resources, training, and mentorship to support their employees' development. They offer challenging assignments, promote learning opportunities, and provide constructive feedback that helps employees expand their skills and capabilities. This commitment to their employees' growth fosters a sense of loyalty, dedication, and engagement.

On the other hand, leaders who hold limiting beliefs about their employees' capabilities may inadvertently demotivate and disengage them. When leaders underestimate their employees' potential or lack confidence in their abilities, it can create a negative perception and low expectations. This can lead to limited opportunities for growth, lack of recognition, and a diminished sense of value among employees. Such beliefs can hinder employees' professional development, restrict their contributions, and ultimately result in disengagement.

Leaders must recognize the influence their beliefs have on employee engagement and actively challenge any limiting beliefs they may hold. By shifting their mindset and embracing a positive belief in their employees' potential, leaders can create an environment that fosters engagement, motivation, and commitment. This involves providing regular feedback and recognition, encouraging open communication, and empowering employees to take ownership of their work. By investing in their employees' growth and supporting their professional development, leaders can inspire a sense of loyalty, dedication, and engagement among their team members.

Leaders' beliefs have a direct impact on employee engagement. When leaders believe in the value and potential of their employees, they create an environment that fosters engagement, motivation, and commitment. By recognizing employees' strengths, providing growth opportunities, and empowering them to take ownership of their work, leaders can inspire a sense of loyalty and dedication. It is essential for leaders to cultivate positive beliefs in their employees' capabilities and provide an environment that nurtures their growth, resulting in increased employee engagement and organizational success.

KEY TAKEAWAY

6. The Role of Personal Growth

Personal growth plays a crucial role in the development and expansion of leaders' belief systems. Leaders who recognize the influence of their beliefs on their actions and outcomes understand the importance of continuously evolving their beliefs to align with new perspectives and insights. They actively engage in self-reflection, seek feedback from others, and challenge their own assumptions and biases. By cultivating a growth mindset, leaders can enhance their leadership effectiveness and increase their ability to achieve desired outcomes.

Engaging in continuous learning is a fundamental aspect of personal growth for leaders. They seek out opportunities to expand their knowledge, skills, and understanding of various subjects. This may involve attending workshops, seminars, or conferences, pursuing further education, or reading books and articles relevant to their field. By continually learning and staying informed, leaders expose themselves to new ideas and perspectives, which can challenge and reshape their existing beliefs.

Seeking feedback is another important component of personal growth for leaders. They actively solicit feedback from their team members, colleagues, mentors, and trusted advisors. Feedback provides valuable insights into blind spots, areas for improvement, and opportunities to align their beliefs with the realities of their environment. By embracing feedback with an open mind, leaders can gain new perspectives and challenge any limiting beliefs they may hold.

Challenging assumptions and biases is essential for leaders to evolve their belief systems. Leaders who are aware of their own biases actively seek to understand and challenge them. They strive to see situations from multiple angles, consider diverse perspectives, and question their own preconceived notions. By challenging assumptions, leaders can develop more inclusive and open-minded beliefs that are responsive to the needs and experiences of their team members and stakeholders.

Cultivating a growth mindset is a foundational element of personal growth for leaders. A growth mindset is the belief that one's abilities and intelligence can be developed through effort, learning, and persistence. Leaders with a growth mindset embrace challenges, view failures as learning opportunities, and have a deep belief in their own and their team's potential for growth and development. By cultivating a growth mindset, leaders create a foundation for continuous learning, resilience, and adaptability, which enables them to evolve their beliefs and approach new challenges with a positive and open mindset.

KEY TAKEAWAY

Personal growth plays a vital role in expanding and evolving leaders' belief systems. Leaders who recognize the influence of their beliefs take intentional steps to engage in continuous learning, seek feedback, challenge assumptions, and cultivate a growth mindset. By actively pursuing personal growth, leaders enhance their leadership effectiveness and increase their ability to achieve desired outcomes. By continuously evolving their beliefs, leaders are better equipped to navigate complex challenges, inspire their teams, and drive positive change within their organizations.

Summary

Leaders cannot escape the results of their beliefs. Beliefs shape leaders' perspectives, decision-making processes, organizational culture, and employee engagement. Positive beliefs can fuel success, while limiting beliefs can hinder growth and achievement. It is essential for leaders to be aware of their beliefs, challenge them when necessary, and cultivate a growth mindset to continuously improve their effectiveness. By aligning their beliefs with their desired outcomes, leaders can create an environment conducive to success, growth, and positive impact.

Leadership
KEY C🔑NCEPTS

17

Time Cannot Be Managed
Leaders Don't Manage Time, They Manage Tasks

Introduction

In the fast-paced world of leadership, time management is often touted as a critical skill for success. However, the concept of "managing time" is misleading. Time is an uncontrollable resource that passes at a constant rate, and no one has the power to manipulate or control it. Instead, effective leaders understand that they cannot manage time itself but rather manage their tasks and activities within the time available. We will explore the idea that leaders don't manage time; they manage tasks and priorities to make the most of the limited time they have.

1. The Nature of Time

Time is an intangible and unyielding resource that governs our lives. It is a constant and impartial force that moves forward without pause, regardless of our desires or efforts. Each individual is granted the same 24 hours in a day, regardless of their status, wealth, or influence. While many speak of "managing time," the reality is that time itself cannot be managed. It progresses at its own pace, remaining consistent and unchangeable.

The Universal Nature of Time: Time is universal in its application. It does not discriminate or favor any individual based on their position, wealth, or influence. Each person experiences time in the same way, with every day comprising 24 hours, 1,440 minutes, and 86,400 seconds. Time operates independently of human desires and efforts, flowing steadily and continuously.

The Inevitability of Time's Progression: Time progresses relentlessly, moving forward without pause or interruption. It cannot be stopped, reversed, or manipulated to fit our preferences. We cannot slow it down when we need more time or speed it up to reach our goals sooner. Time remains steadfast and consistent, unaffected by our attempts to manage or control it.

Rethinking the Concept of "Managing Time": While the concept of managing time has become deeply ingrained in our language and practices, it is essential to recognize the inherent limitations in this notion. We cannot manage time itself, as it operates independently of our actions and intentions. Instead, we must shift our focus to managing our actions, priorities, and behaviors within the constraints of time.

Task and Priority Management: Effective leaders understand that they cannot manage time, but they can manage their tasks and priorities within the time available. They recognize the importance of setting clear goals, identifying key tasks, and prioritizing their actions based on their significance and urgency. By focusing on task and priority management, leaders can optimize their productivity and allocate their time and resources more effectively.

Efficient Time Allocation: Leaders who grasp the concept of managing tasks rather than time understand the importance of efficient time allocation. They allocate their time based on the value and impact of each task. By identifying high-priority tasks that align with their goals and utilizing their time wisely, leaders can maximize their productivity and achieve desired outcomes.

Planning and Time Optimization: To effectively manage tasks within the constraints of time, leaders engage in careful planning and time optimization. They establish realistic timelines, set deadlines, and create schedules that account for the necessary time and resources required for each task. Through effective planning, leaders can make the most of the available time and ensure that important tasks are completed efficiently.

Time is an unchangeable and impartial resource that operates independently of human influence. It progresses at a constant pace, offering each individual the same amount of time in a day. The concept of "managing time" is inherently flawed as time cannot be manipulated or controlled. Instead, leaders must focus on managing their actions, priorities, and behaviors within the constraints of time. By embracing task and priority management, leaders can optimize their productivity, allocate their time effectively, and achieve desired outcomes. It is through effective task management and efficient time allocation that leaders can navigate the constraints of time and drive success in their personal and professional endeavors.

KEY TAKEAWAY

2. Task Management:

Task management is a crucial aspect of effective leadership. Leaders understand that time itself cannot be managed, but they can manage their tasks and activities within the time available. By focusing on task management, leaders can optimize their productivity, achieve desired outcomes, and make efficient use of their limited time.

Setting Priorities: Leaders recognize the importance of setting priorities to effectively manage their tasks. They understand that not all tasks carry the same level of importance or urgency. By identifying and categorizing tasks based on their significance, leaders can allocate their time and resources accordingly. Prioritization allows leaders to focus their attention on high-impact tasks that align with their goals and contribute the most value to their organization.

Organizing Workload: Effective leaders understand the significance of organizing their workload. They break down larger tasks into smaller, manageable components, making them more approachable and easier to accomplish. By organizing their tasks, leaders can develop a clear roadmap of what needs to be done, ensuring that nothing falls through the cracks. This helps to streamline their workflow, improve efficiency, and reduce the risk of overlooking important tasks.

Allocating Time: Leaders understand the importance of allocating time to different tasks based on their priorities. They recognize that time is a finite resource and must be utilized judiciously. By assigning specific time slots or time blocks to each task, leaders can create a structured schedule that ensures progress is made on important tasks. Effective time allocation helps leaders make the most of their available time and avoid procrastination or time-wasting activities.

Delegating and Outsourcing: Leaders understand that they cannot do everything themselves. They recognize the value of delegation and outsourcing tasks to others who have the necessary skills and expertise. By effectively delegating tasks, leaders can free up their own time to focus on higher-level strategic activities that require their attention. Delegation also empowers team members, fosters their professional growth, and promotes a sense of ownership and accountability within the team.

Effective Communication and Collaboration: Leaders understand that effective communication and collaboration are essential for task management. They establish clear lines of communication, ensuring that team members have a shared understanding of tasks, expectations, and deadlines. Leaders promote a collaborative environment where team members can work together, share insights, and support one another in accomplishing their tasks. This encourages a sense of collective responsibility and enhances the overall efficiency and productivity of the team.

Regular Evaluation and Adaptation: Leaders understand that task management is an ongoing process that requires regular evaluation and adaptation. They periodically review their task management strategies, reflecting on what worked well and identifying areas for improvement. Leaders are open to feedback and seek opportunities to refine their approach, leveraging new tools, technologies, or methodologies that can enhance their task management practices.

KEY TAKEAWAY

Leaders understand that effective leadership requires managing tasks and activities within the time available. By setting priorities, organizing their workload, allocating time wisely, and delegating when necessary, leaders can optimize their productivity and achieve desired outcomes. Effective task management enables leaders to make efficient use of their limited time, ensuring that important tasks are accomplished, deadlines are met, and goals are achieved. By focusing on task management, leaders can drive success, foster productivity, and inspire their teams to accomplish their collective objectives.

3. Prioritization and Time Allocation

Prioritization and time allocation are critical skills for effective leaders. By prioritizing tasks and allocating time wisely, leaders ensure that their efforts are directed towards activities that align with organizational goals and objectives. This allows them to maximize their impact and make the most efficient use of their time. Here are some key considerations for leaders when it comes to prioritization and time allocation:

Identify High-Priority Tasks: Leaders must first identify and distinguish high-priority tasks from lower-priority ones. This involves understanding the strategic objectives of the organization and aligning tasks with those objectives. By focusing on high-priority tasks, leaders ensure that their efforts contribute directly to the overall success of the organization.

Consider Urgency and Deadlines: In addition to importance, leaders should consider the urgency and deadlines associated with each task. Tasks that have imminent deadlines or time-sensitive requirements should be given priority to avoid any negative impact on project timelines or organizational outcomes. Leaders must assess the urgency of tasks and allocate sufficient time to complete them in a timely manner.

Evaluate Resource Availability: Leaders must consider the availability of resources, such as manpower, budget, or equipment, when prioritizing tasks. If certain tasks require specific resources that are limited or not readily available, leaders may need to adjust their priorities or allocate additional time to secure the necessary resources. This ensures that tasks can be completed effectively and without unnecessary delays.

Assess Strategic Significance: Leaders should assess the strategic significance of each task and how it contributes to the long-term goals of the organization. Some tasks may have a higher impact on organizational success, while others may be less critical. By allocating more time and resources to tasks that align with the organization's strategic priorities, leaders can maximize their efforts and ensure that they are moving the organization forward.

Delegate and Empower: Leaders should delegate tasks whenever possible, especially those that can be handled by team members with the necessary skills and expertise. Delegation not only helps distribute the workload but also empowers team members to take ownership and develop their capabilities. By effectively delegating tasks, leaders free up their own time to focus on higher-level responsibilities and strategic initiatives.

Flexibility and Adaptability: Leaders must be flexible and adaptable in their approach to task prioritization and time allocation. Circumstances may change, new opportunities may arise, or unexpected challenges may occur. Leaders should be willing to reassess and adjust their priorities and time allocation accordingly. This flexibility allows them to respond to evolving situations and ensure that their efforts remain aligned with the most current needs and priorities.

KEY TAKEAWAY

Prioritization and time allocation are vital skills for leaders. By identifying high-priority tasks, considering urgency and deadlines, evaluating resource availability, assessing strategic significance, delegating effectively, and remaining flexible, leaders can optimize their productivity and ensure that their time is invested in activities that have the greatest impact on organizational success. Effective prioritization and time allocation contribute to the efficient use of resources, the achievement of goals, and the overall effectiveness of leaders in their roles.

4. Delegation and Time Optimization:

Delegation and time optimization are essential strategies for effective leaders. By recognizing the value of delegation, leaders can leverage the skills and capabilities of their team members, freeing up their own time for more strategic and high-value activities. Here are some key points to consider when it comes to delegation and time optimization:

Assessing Task Suitability: Leaders must assess tasks to determine which ones can be effectively delegated. Tasks that do not require their specific expertise or decision-making authority are prime candidates for delegation. Leaders should consider the skill sets, capabilities, and workload of team members to identify suitable individuals who can handle delegated tasks efficiently.

Clear Communication and Expectations: To ensure successful delegation, leaders must clearly communicate their expectations regarding the task, desired outcomes, and any relevant deadlines. Effective communication helps avoid misunderstandings and ensures that team members understand the purpose and importance of the delegated tasks. Clear expectations enable team members to take ownership and work independently, reducing the need for constant supervision.

Selecting the Right Team Members: Leaders must identify team members who have the necessary skills, knowledge, and capabilities to handle delegated tasks effectively. By matching the strengths and abilities of team members with the requirements of the tasks, leaders can optimize the delegation process. This not only ensures that tasks are completed successfully but also provides opportunities for team members to develop new skills and grow professionally.

Providing Support and Resources: Leaders should provide the necessary support, guidance, and resources to enable team members to complete delegated tasks successfully. This may involve providing access to relevant information, offering training or mentorship, or ensuring that team members have the required tools and resources to carry out their responsibilities. By providing support, leaders empower team members to take ownership and excel in their delegated tasks.

Trust and Empowerment: Leaders must trust their team members' abilities and empower them to make decisions and take ownership of their delegated tasks. By delegating responsibilities, leaders demonstrate confidence in their team members' capabilities, which not only boosts morale but also fosters a sense of ownership and accountability. Trust and empowerment motivate team members to perform at their best, leading to improved productivity and efficiency.

Regular Feedback and Recognition: Leaders should provide regular feedback and recognition to their team members for their delegated tasks. Feedback helps ensure that tasks are on track and provides an opportunity for course correction if needed. Recognizing the efforts and achievements of team members reinforces their value and encourages continued growth and development.

Delegation and time optimization are critical strategies for effective leaders. By delegating tasks to capable team members, leaders can optimize their use of time, allowing them to focus on higher-value activities and strategic decision-making. Effective delegation empowers team members, fosters their growth and development, and improves overall team productivity. Through clear communication, selecting the right team members, providing support and resources, building trust and empowerment, and offering feedback and recognition, leaders can ensure successful delegation and maximize their own and their team's effectiveness.

5. Time Management Tools and Techniques

Time management tools and techniques play a vital role in helping leaders manage their tasks and activities effectively. These tools provide structure, organization, and support, enabling leaders to optimize their productivity and make efficient use of their time. Here are some commonly used time management tools and techniques:

Time Tracking Apps: Time tracking apps help leaders monitor and analyze how they allocate their time. These apps allow leaders to record the time spent on various tasks, projects, or activities. By tracking their time, leaders can gain insights into their work patterns, identify time-wasting activities, and make informed decisions about task prioritization and resource allocation.

Calendars and Scheduling: Calendars are essential tools for leaders to manage their time. Whether in digital or physical form, calendars enable leaders to schedule their tasks, appointments, and meetings. By visually organizing their time, leaders can gain a clear overview of their commitments, avoid double bookings, and allocate appropriate time for each task or event. Reminders and notifications help leaders stay on track and meet deadlines.

To-Do Lists: To-do lists are simple yet effective tools for managing tasks and activities. Leaders can create lists of tasks, prioritize them, and check them off as they are completed. To-do lists provide a visual representation of the tasks that need to be accomplished, ensuring that nothing is overlooked. They help leaders stay focused, organized, and on top of their responsibilities.

Project Management Software: For leaders managing complex projects or teams, project management software can be invaluable. These tools offer features such as task assignment, progress tracking, document sharing, and collaboration. Project management software helps leaders plan, monitor, and control project activities, ensuring that tasks are completed within the specified timeframes and that team members have a clear understanding of their responsibilities.

Time Blocking: Time blocking is a technique that involves scheduling specific blocks of time for specific tasks or activities. Leaders allocate dedicated time slots in their calendar for focused work, meetings, or other activities. By setting aside uninterrupted time for specific tasks, leaders can enhance their concentration, reduce distractions, and ensure that important work receives the attention it deserves.

Pomodoro Technique: The Pomodoro Technique is a time management technique that involves working in focused intervals, typically 25 minutes, followed by short breaks. Leaders set a timer for each work interval and commit to working on a specific task during that time. After each work interval, they take a short break before starting the next one. This technique helps maintain focus, manage energy levels, and enhance productivity.

Time management tools and techniques provide leaders with the structure, organization, and support needed to effectively manage their tasks and activities. Whether it's time tracking apps, calendars, to-do lists, project management software, time blocking, or the Pomodoro Technique, these tools and techniques help leaders stay organized, prioritize tasks, and manage deadlines. By leveraging these tools, leaders can make the most efficient use of their time, remain focused on their goals, and optimize their productivity and effectiveness.

KEY TAKEAWAY

---

6. Continuous Learning and Adaptation

Continuous learning and adaptation are crucial for leaders in their journey of managing tasks and priorities effectively. Leaders understand that the dynamics of their work environment, the demands placed upon them, and the nature of their tasks can evolve over time. To stay ahead and optimize their performance, leaders embrace continuous learning and adapt their approach to task management. Here are some key aspects of continuous learning and adaptation for effective task management:

Reflecting on Effectiveness: Leaders take time to reflect on their task management practices and evaluate their effectiveness. They assess the outcomes achieved, the efficiency of their processes, and any areas for improvement. Reflection allows leaders to gain insights into their strengths and weaknesses, identify patterns, and make informed decisions about adjustments needed in their task management approach.

Seeking Feedback: Leaders actively seek feedback from colleagues, team members, and stakeholders to gain different perspectives and insights. They encourage open and honest communication, inviting suggestions and critiques regarding their task management practices. Feedback provides valuable information that leaders can use to refine their strategies, improve their efficiency, and align their practices with the needs and expectations of others.

Embracing New Tools and Techniques: Leaders stay updated with emerging tools, techniques, and technologies related to task management. They explore and adopt new methods that can enhance their productivity, organization, and time optimization. Whether it's implementing new software, leveraging automation, or adopting innovative strategies, leaders are open to incorporating tools and techniques that align with their goals and facilitate effective task management.

Professional Development: Leaders invest in their own professional development, seeking opportunities to expand their knowledge and skills in task management. They attend seminars, workshops, and conferences related to time management, organizational skills, and productivity enhancement. By staying informed and learning from experts in the field, leaders can acquire new perspectives and best practices to refine their task management approach.

Flexibility and Adaptability: Leaders understand the importance of being flexible and adaptable in their task management practices. They recognize that circumstances may change, priorities may shift, and unexpected challenges may arise. By embracing adaptability, leaders can adjust their plans, reprioritize tasks, and reallocate resources as needed. This flexibility allows leaders to respond effectively to evolving situations and maintain productivity in the face of change.

Encouraging a Learning Culture: Effective leaders foster a learning culture within their teams and organizations. They encourage team members to engage in continuous learning, share best practices, and contribute ideas for improving task management processes. By fostering a culture of learning and innovation, leaders create an environment where everyone is encouraged to adapt, grow, and optimize their task management skills.

Continuous learning and adaptation are essential for effective task management. Leaders reflect on their effectiveness, seek feedback, embrace new tools and techniques, invest in professional development, remain flexible and adaptable, and foster a learning culture. By continuously improving their task management practices, leaders can enhance their efficiency, optimize their time allocation, and achieve their goals with greater effectiveness.

KEY TAKEAWAY

Summary

Time cannot be managed by leaders or anyone else, as it progresses at a constant rate beyond human control. However, leaders can effectively manage their tasks and activities within the time available. By prioritizing tasks, allocating time wisely, delegating responsibilities, and utilizing time management tools, leaders can optimize their productivity and achieve desired outcomes. Recognizing the distinction between managing time and managing tasks is crucial for leaders to make the most efficient use of their limited time and drive success in their personal and professional endeavors.

Leadership
KEY C⊙NCEPTS

18

It Is What It Is
Nothing Is Good or Bad Until You Relate It to Something Else

Introduction

In the realm of leadership, perceptions and interpretations play a significant role in shaping our understanding of situations and events. Often, we tend to label things as either good or bad based on our subjective assessments. However, effective leaders understand that reality is complex and that labeling something as inherently good or bad can limit our understanding and hinder our ability to navigate challenges and opportunities. We will explore the notion that nothing is inherently good or bad until we relate it to something else and how this perspective can enhance leadership effectiveness.

1. The Subjectivity of Good and Bad

In the realm of leadership, the subjectivity of good and bad is a fundamental concept that effective leaders grasp. They understand that individuals bring their own unique perspectives and interpretations to any given situation. What may be considered good or bad is inherently influenced by personal experiences, beliefs, values, and cultural backgrounds.

Leaders recognize that their own perceptions of good and bad may differ from those of their team members or stakeholders. They acknowledge that these subjective assessments can shape their decision-making, communication, and overall leadership approach. By embracing the subjectivity of good and bad, leaders create an inclusive environment that values diverse perspectives and encourages open dialogue.

Leaders also understand that objective reality exists beyond individual viewpoints. They recognize that their own perceptions may be limited and that considering multiple perspectives is essential for gaining a comprehensive understanding of a situation. This broader perspective allows leaders to make more informed decisions and develop strategies that take into account a wider range of potential outcomes and impacts.

By actively seeking out and considering different viewpoints, leaders can cultivate empathy, enhance their cultural intelligence, and promote a more inclusive and collaborative work environment. They encourage their team members to share their perspectives, fostering an atmosphere of psychological safety where diverse opinions are valued and respected.

Leaders who appreciate the subjectivity of good and bad also recognize the importance of self-awareness. They continuously reflect on their own biases and beliefs, examining how these subjective factors influence their perception and evaluation of situations. This self-awareness allows leaders to approach decision-making with a more objective and rational mindset, reducing the risk of being swayed solely by personal preferences or preconceived notions of good and bad.

KEY TAKEAWAY

Leaders who acknowledge the subjectivity of good and bad understand that different individuals may perceive situations differently based on their personal experiences, beliefs, values, and cultural backgrounds. By embracing this subjectivity, leaders foster an inclusive and diverse work environment, encourage open dialogue, and make more informed decisions that consider multiple perspectives. Through self-awareness and a commitment to understanding objective reality beyond their own viewpoint, leaders can effectively navigate complex challenges and inspire their teams to achieve collective success.

2. Context and Relativity

Leadership is not a one-size-fits-all approach, and effective leaders understand the importance of considering the context and relativity of situations. They recognize that the interpretation of events is highly influenced by the specific circumstances and conditions in which they occur. By acknowledging the relativity of situations, leaders can adopt a more nuanced and adaptive approach to their decision-making and actions.

Context refers to the unique set of circumstances, factors, and conditions that surround a particular situation. It includes factors such as the organizational culture, industry trends, economic climate, stakeholder dynamics, and internal and external influences. Leaders understand that these contextual elements significantly shape the outcomes and consequences of their actions.

Effective leaders approach situations with an open mind, recognizing that what may appear negative or challenging at first glance may actually present unforeseen opportunities or possibilities. They understand that setbacks or obstacles can serve as catalysts for growth, learning, and innovation. By reframing challenges as opportunities, leaders can unlock new pathways and solutions that lead to positive outcomes.

On the other hand, leaders also recognize that what may seem positive initially may have hidden drawbacks or unintended consequences. They exercise caution and critically evaluate the potential risks and long-term implications of their decisions. Leaders avoid being swayed solely by surface-level appearances and take a holistic view of the situation.

By considering the context and relativity of a situation, leaders demonstrate their ability to adapt their strategies and approaches based on the specific circumstances. They gather relevant information, seek diverse perspectives, and make informed decisions that are tailored to the unique context at hand.

Leaders who understand the relativity of situations also foster an environment that encourages open dialogue and feedback. They recognize that different individuals may have varying perspectives based on their roles, experiences, and expertise. By actively seeking out diverse viewpoints, leaders can gain a more comprehensive understanding of the context and make more informed decisions that consider the interests and needs of all stakeholders.

KEY TAKEAWAY

Effective leaders understand that the context and relativity of situations significantly influence the interpretation and assessment of their goodness or badness. By approaching situations with an open mind, reframing challenges as opportunities, and critically evaluating the potential risks and consequences, leaders can make informed decisions that lead to positive outcomes. By considering the context and embracing relativity, leaders can navigate complexities, adapt their strategies, and inspire their teams to achieve success in a dynamic and ever-changing environment.

3. Growth and Learning from Challenges

Leadership is not immune to challenges and setbacks, but effective leaders have a unique perspective on how they approach and respond to these difficulties. Rather than labeling challenges as inherently bad, leaders view them as valuable opportunities for growth and learning. They recognize that adversity has the potential to foster resilience, enhance adaptability, and promote personal and professional development.

Leaders understand that challenges can provide valuable lessons and insights that contribute to their own growth and the growth of their teams. They approach these challenges with a mindset that is open to learning and extracting meaningful takeaways. They seek to understand the root causes of the challenges, analyze the contributing factors, and identify areas for improvement.

By reframing challenges as learning experiences, leaders foster resilience within themselves and their teams. They encourage their team members to embrace challenges as opportunities for growth and provide support and resources to facilitate learning and development. Leaders promote a culture that values continuous improvement, experimentation, and a willingness to learn from failures.

Through challenges, leaders discover new perspectives, innovative solutions, and alternative approaches. They encourage their teams to think creatively and find opportunities for improvement and innovation amidst adversity. By fostering a growth mindset, leaders empower their teams to view challenges as stepping stones to success rather than insurmountable obstacles.

Effective leaders provide a good example and actively participate in self-reflection and self-improvement. They are not afraid to admit mistakes, take ownership of their actions, and seek opportunities for personal growth. They constantly seek feedback and leverage challenging situations to refine their leadership skills, expand their knowledge, and enhance their effectiveness.

Leaders who embrace challenges as opportunities for growth and learning inspire their teams to adopt the same mindset. They create an environment that encourages experimentation, curiosity, and resilience. By providing support, resources, and a safe space for failure, leaders foster a culture that values continuous learning, adaptability, and innovation.

Leaders who view challenges as opportunities for growth and learning foster resilience, adaptability, and a growth mindset within themselves and their teams. By reframing challenges as learning experiences, leaders promote personal and professional development, encourage innovative thinking, and create a culture of continuous improvement. Through their positive mindset and approach to challenges, leaders inspire their teams to embrace difficulties as stepping stones toward success and create an environment that thrives on learning and growth.

KEY TAKEAWAY

4. Managing Perceptions and Emotions:

The ability to manage perceptions and emotions is a crucial skill for effective leaders. They understand that how they interpret and relate to situations directly impacts their emotional responses, attitudes, and subsequent actions. By actively reframing events and examining them from different perspectives, leaders can manage their own perceptions and emotional reactions, leading to a more balanced and objective approach.

Leaders recognize that their initial interpretations of events may be influenced by biases, assumptions, and personal experiences. They understand that these subjective filters can cloud their judgment and hinder their ability to make rational and informed decisions. Therefore, they make a conscious effort to challenge their initial perceptions and consider alternative viewpoints.

By reframing events, leaders shift their perspective and examine the situation from different angles. They question their assumptions, seek additional information, and consider various factors that may influence the situation. This process helps them gain a more comprehensive understanding and reduces the impact of personal biases on their perceptions.

Managing perceptions also involves maintaining a sense of objectivity and avoiding knee-jerk reactions. Effective leaders understand the importance of staying calm and composed, especially in challenging or high-pressure situations. They recognize that their emotional state can influence their decision-making and the way they communicate with others.

To manage their emotions, leaders employ various strategies such as deep breathing, self-reflection, and seeking support from trusted colleagues or mentors. They practice emotional intelligence, which involves recognizing and understanding their emotions, as well as those of others. By regulating their emotions, leaders can respond to situations in a constructive and balanced manner.

Leaders understand that their emotional state can have a ripple effect on their teams. By managing their own emotions, they create a positive and supportive work environment. They model resilience, adaptability, and a solution-oriented mindset, inspiring their team members to approach challenges with a similar perspective.

Effective leaders also recognize the importance of clear and effective communication. They understand that their words and actions can shape the perceptions of others. By conveying information accurately, empathetically, and transparently, leaders can influence the perceptions of their team members and stakeholders, fostering trust and understanding.

KEY TAKEAWAY

Effective leaders understand that managing perceptions and emotions is crucial for maintaining a balanced and objective approach. By actively reframing events, examining situations from different perspectives, and managing their own emotions, leaders can make rational and informed decisions. They create a positive work environment, inspire their teams, and foster effective communication. By managing their own perceptions and emotions, leaders enhance their leadership effectiveness and create a culture that promotes resilience, adaptability, and constructive problem-solving.

6. Embracing the Complexity of Reality

In the realm of leadership, effective leaders recognize and embrace the inherent complexity of reality. They understand that situations, events, and issues are rarely black and white, and oversimplifying them as purely good or bad can hinder their ability to make informed decisions and navigate complex challenges. Instead, leaders appreciate the multifaceted nature of reality and engage in a more nuanced and holistic analysis.

Leaders acknowledge that in any given situation, there are often multiple factors, perspectives, and influences at play. They resist the temptation to rely on simplistic dichotomies and binary thinking, which can lead to limited understanding and ineffective decision-making. Instead, they take the time to gather information, seek diverse perspectives, and consider various dimensions of the situation.

By embracing the complexity of reality, leaders foster a more comprehensive understanding of the dynamics involved. They recognize that positive and negative elements can coexist within a given situation. This understanding allows them to identify and leverage the strengths and opportunities while acknowledging and addressing the challenges and risks.

Leaders also appreciate that complex situations require a holistic analysis, taking into account the interrelationships and interconnectedness of various factors. They understand that a reductionist approach, focusing on isolated components, may fail to capture the full picture. Therefore, leaders engage in systems thinking, considering the broader context and understanding how different elements interact and influence one another.

By embracing complexity, leaders encourage critical thinking and creativity within their teams. They create an environment that values diverse perspectives, encourages open dialogue, and fosters innovative solutions. They recognize that complex problems often require collaborative efforts, drawing on the collective intelligence and expertise of their team members.

Leaders who embrace complexity are comfortable with ambiguity and uncertainty. They understand that not all aspects of a situation can be fully known or predicted. They demonstrate adaptability and agility, adjusting their strategies and approaches as new information becomes available or as the situation evolves.

> *Effective leaders appreciate and embrace the complexity of reality. They resist the temptation to*

oversimplify situations as purely good or bad and engage in a more nuanced and holistic analysis. By acknowledging the multifaceted nature of events, considering diverse perspectives, and understanding the interrelationships between various factors, leaders make informed decisions and navigate complex challenges more effectively. They foster a culture of critical thinking, creativity, and adaptability, enabling their teams to thrive in an ever-changing and complex world.

7. Optimizing Outcomes

Effective leaders understand the importance of optimizing outcomes by adopting a flexible and solution-oriented mindset. Rather than immediately labeling events as good or bad, leaders approach situations with an open mind and a focus on finding the best possible outcome. By refraining from rigid thinking and embracing flexibility, leaders can explore opportunities, encourage collaboration, and foster innovation.

When faced with a challenge or opportunity, leaders resist the urge to jump to conclusions or make hasty judgments. They understand that taking a step back, gathering information, and considering various perspectives is essential to fully understanding the situation. This enables them to identify the potential for growth and improvement, even in seemingly unfavorable circumstances.

By maintaining a solution-oriented mindset, leaders actively seek opportunities for growth and improvement. They view setbacks and obstacles as learning experiences and stepping stones toward achieving their goals. Rather than dwelling on the negative aspects of a situation, they focus on identifying creative solutions and innovative approaches that can lead to optimal outcomes.

Effective leaders also understand the value of collaboration. They actively seek input and ideas from their team members, recognizing that diverse perspectives can lead to more robust solutions. By creating an inclusive environment that encourages the sharing of ideas and the exchange of feedback, leaders tap into the collective intelligence and creativity of their teams.

In addition, leaders encourage a culture of innovation by promoting an open-minded and risk-tolerant environment. They inspire their teams to think outside the box, challenge the status quo, and explore unconventional approaches. By embracing innovative thinking, leaders can uncover new possibilities and uncover opportunities that may have been overlooked.

Flexibility is another key attribute of leaders who optimize outcomes. They understand that circumstances can change, and strategies may need to be adjusted accordingly. They remain adaptable and open to new information, allowing them to make informed decisions based on the evolving context.

By adopting a flexible and open-minded perspective, leaders capitalize on the unique characteristics of each situation. They recognize that what works in one scenario may not work in another, and they tailor their approaches accordingly. This enables them to leverage the strengths and opportunities present in a given situation, leading to outcomes that maximize success.

Effective leaders refrain from immediately labeling events as good or bad and instead approach situations with a solution-oriented mindset. By maintaining flexibility, encouraging collaboration and innovation, and capitalizing on the unique characteristics of each situation, leaders optimize outcomes and achieve success. They foster a culture that embraces growth, creativity, and continuous improvement, driving their teams to reach their full potential.

KEY TAKEAWAY

Summary

Leaders who understand that nothing is inherently good or bad until related to something else exhibit a more nuanced and adaptable approach to leadership. By recognizing the subjectivity of perceptions, understanding the impact of context, embracing challenges as opportunities for growth, managing their own perceptions and emotions, appreciating the complexity of reality, and optimizing outcomes, leaders can navigate uncertainty with confidence and guide their teams towards success. By adopting this perspective, leaders can foster a culture of resilience, adaptability, and continuous learning, enabling themselves and their organizations to thrive in an ever-changing world.

Leadership

Do The Next Right Thing
When A Leader's Values Are Clear Their Choices Are Easy

Introduction

Leadership is inherently about making choices and decisions that shape the path of an organization or team. Effective leaders understand the importance of clarity in their values as a guiding compass for decision-making. When a leader's values are clear, their choices become easier and more aligned with their principles. We will explore the significance of clear values in leadership and how they simplify decision-making processes.

1. Defining Values

In the realm of leadership, values play a critical role in shaping the actions, decisions, and overall direction of a leader. When a leader's values are clear and well-defined, they serve as a guiding force, providing a foundation for decision-making. This paper explores the importance of defining values in leadership and how they influence a leader's choices.

Defining Values: Values are deeply held beliefs and principles that guide an individual's behavior and decision-making. They serve as a moral compass, shaping the way leaders perceive and respond to various situations. Values can encompass a wide range of aspects, including honesty, integrity, respect, empathy, accountability, teamwork, innovation, and more. When values are clearly defined, they provide a framework for ethical and purpose-driven decision-making.

Alignment with Core Principles: When a leader's values are clear, they act as a guiding force, ensuring that decisions and actions are in line with their core principles. Leaders with well-defined values are aware of what matters most to them and use this awareness to guide their choices. By aligning their actions with their values, leaders maintain integrity and authenticity, inspiring trust and confidence in their leadership.

Ethical Decision-Making: Values play a crucial role in ethical decision-making. Clear values provide leaders with a moral framework to evaluate options and make choices that align with their principles. When faced with ethical dilemmas, leaders with defined values can refer to their core beliefs to guide their decisions. Values act as a compass that helps leaders navigate complex situations while staying true to their ethical principles.

Consistency and Trust: Leaders who have clear values exhibit consistency in their decision-making and actions. This consistency reinforces their credibility and builds trust among their team members and stakeholders. When leaders consistently make choices that align with their values, they establish a sense of reliability and predictability. This fosters an environment of trust, where individuals feel secure in their leader's commitment to ethical behavior and principled decision-making.

Influence on Organizational Culture: Values also play a significant role in shaping the culture of an organization. When leaders define and live their values, they create a ripple effect that permeates the entire organization. Values become the guiding principles for the behavior, actions, and decisions of all team members. A strong alignment between individual and organizational values leads to a cohesive and purpose-driven culture where everyone is working towards shared goals and making choices that reflect the core principles.

Communication and Transparency: Defining values promotes effective communication and transparency within the organization. When leaders openly communicate their values, they provide clarity on the principles that guide their decisions. This transparency fosters trust and encourages open dialogue, as team members feel empowered to express their opinions and contribute to decision-making processes. Values become a shared language that unifies individuals and promotes a culture of collaboration and mutual respect.

Defining values is a crucial aspect of effective leadership. When a leader's values are clear, they act as a moral compass, guiding decision-making and shaping the overall direction of the leader and the organization. Values provide a framework for ethical decision-making, foster consistency and trust, influence organizational culture, and promote effective communication. By defining and living their values, leaders establish a strong foundation for principled leadership and inspire others to make choices that align with shared principles.

KEY TAKEAWAY

2. Guiding Principles

Values serve as guiding principles for leaders, providing a framework for decision-making and shaping their overall leadership approach. When leaders have clearly defined values, they act as a reference point that helps guide their choices and actions. This paper explores the significance of guiding principles in leadership and how they contribute to consistency, integrity, and trust.

Establishing Consistency: Clearly defined values establish a foundation of consistency in a leader's decision-making processes. Values serve as a benchmark against which leaders can evaluate options and determine the most aligned course of action. By consistently aligning their decisions with their values, leaders demonstrate a sense of purpose and integrity, which fosters trust among team members and stakeholders. Consistency in decision-making enhances credibility and reinforces a leader's commitment to their principles.

Strengthening Integrity: Values act as a compass that guides leaders to make choices that align with their core principles. When leaders adhere to their values, even in challenging or uncertain circumstances, they demonstrate integrity and ethical behavior. The consistent application of values ensures that decisions are made in alignment with what the leader believes is right and just. By upholding their values, leaders build trust and establish a reputation for integrity, inspiring confidence in their leadership.

Ethical Decision-Making: Guiding principles derived from values play a crucial role in ethical decision-making. Values serve as a moral compass, helping leaders assess the ethical implications of their choices. When faced with complex dilemmas, leaders refer to their values to evaluate options and determine the most ethical course of action. By adhering to their values, leaders ensure that their decisions are consistent with their ethical beliefs and contribute to the greater good.

Inspiring Trust and Credibility: Leaders who consistently make decisions based on their guiding principles establish trust and credibility among their team members and stakeholders. When team members observe leaders adhering to their values, they develop confidence in their decision-making and trust in their leadership. The consistent application of values creates a sense of predictability and reliability, providing a foundation for effective teamwork, collaboration, and organizational success.

Alignment with Organizational Culture: Guiding principles derived from values also play a significant role in shaping the organizational culture. When leaders consistently uphold their values, they set an example for others to follow. This alignment between the leader's values and the organization's values establishes a cohesive and purpose-driven culture. Team members are more likely to align their actions and decisions with the organization's values when they witness leaders consistently applying their guiding principles.

Building Meaningful Relationships: Leaders who adhere to their guiding principles foster meaningful relationships with their team members and stakeholders. The consistency and integrity displayed in decision-making build trust and rapport. When leaders prioritize their values, they create an environment where individuals feel safe and valued. This encourages open communication, collaboration, and a shared commitment to organizational success.

KEY TAKEAWAY

Guiding principles derived from clearly defined values are essential in leadership. They provide leaders with a framework for decision-making, ensuring consistency, integrity, and ethical behavior. Leaders who consistently align their actions with their guiding principles inspire trust and credibility among their team members and stakeholders. These guiding principles also shape the organizational culture, fostering an environment of collaboration, shared values, and ethical behavior. By adhering to their values, leaders establish a strong foundation for effective leadership, driving organizational success and creating meaningful relationships.

3. Streamlining Decision-Making

Effective decision-making is a critical aspect of leadership, and clear values play a significant role in streamlining this process. When leaders have well-defined values, they provide a framework that simplifies decision-making by offering a set of guiding principles. This paper explores how clear values streamline decision-making for leaders and enable them to make choices that align with their principles.

Clarity in Priorities: Clear values provide leaders with a sense of clarity in determining their priorities. When faced with multiple options or conflicting demands, leaders can refer to their values to identify which choices are most aligned with their principles. Values act as a filter that helps leaders assess the importance and relevance of each option, making it easier to prioritize and allocate resources effectively.

Evaluation of Impact: Values serve as a reference point for evaluating the potential impact of decisions on stakeholders and the broader organization. Leaders can assess the consequences of their choices by considering whether they align with their values and contribute to the overall mission and vision. This evaluation helps leaders make informed decisions that have a positive and meaningful impact on the individuals and communities they serve.

Alignment with Ethical Principles: Clear values provide leaders with a moral compass to navigate ethical dilemmas and complex situations. By referring to their values, leaders can assess the ethical implications of different options and choose the course of action that is most aligned with their principles. Values act as a guide in ensuring that decisions are made with integrity, transparency, and respect for ethical standards.

Consistency in Decision-Making: Values contribute to the consistency of decision-making. When leaders have clear values, they can make choices that are consistent with their principles and previous decisions. This consistency builds trust among team members, stakeholders, and the wider organization, as it demonstrates a reliable decision-making approach. Clear values prevent leaders from being swayed by short-term gains or external pressures, allowing them to stay true to their principles over time.

Streamlined Evaluation Process: Clear values streamline the evaluation process by providing a benchmark against which options can be assessed. Leaders can quickly determine whether a choice aligns with their values, reducing the time and effort required to analyze each option. This streamlined evaluation process enables leaders to make decisions more efficiently, especially in time-sensitive situations.

Enhanced Decision-Making Confidence: When leaders have clear values, they gain confidence in their decision-making. They trust their principles and rely on them as a foundation for making choices. This confidence enables leaders to act decisively, even in challenging circumstances, as they have a clear reference point for evaluating options. The assurance that their decisions align with their values bolsters their confidence in their leadership abilities.

KEY TAKEAWAY

Clear values simplify decision-making for leaders by providing a framework to evaluate choices. They enable leaders to prioritize effectively, evaluate the impact of decisions, align with ethical principles, and ensure consistency. By streamlining the evaluation process and enhancing decision-making confidence, clear values empower leaders to make choices that are in line with their principles and contribute to the long-term success and well-being of their organizations.

4. Strengthening Leadership Authenticity

Leaders who prioritize authenticity understand the importance of aligning their values with their actions and decisions. They take the time to reflect on their core beliefs and principles and ensure that they are consistently reflected in their behavior.

Authentic leaders do not compromise their values for short-term gains or external pressures. Instead, they remain true to themselves and their convictions, even when faced with difficult choices or challenging situations. This consistency in their behavior creates a sense of trust and reliability, as team members and stakeholders know they can rely on the leader to act in line with their values.

Leaders who prioritize authenticity also communicate openly and honestly with their team members and stakeholders. They share their thoughts, ideas, and concerns in a transparent manner, fostering a culture of trust and open dialogue. By being genuine and vulnerable in their communication, leaders encourage others to do the same, promoting a climate of authenticity and mutual respect.

Furthermore, leaders who prioritize authenticity build meaningful relationships with their team members. They take the time to understand their strengths, aspirations, and challenges, and provide support and guidance accordingly. By showing empathy, listening actively, and demonstrating genuine care for the well-being of their team members, leaders foster a sense of trust and create a positive work environment.

Authentic leaders also acknowledge and learn from their mistakes. They take responsibility for their actions and are willing to admit when they are wrong. By modeling accountability and humility, they create an environment where learning and growth are valued, and individuals are encouraged to take risks and learn from their experiences.

Leaders who prioritize authenticity strengthen their leadership by aligning their values with their actions, communicating openly and honestly, building meaningful relationships, and demonstrating accountability and humility. By embracing their authentic selves, leaders create an environment of trust, respect, and growth, where individuals can thrive and contribute their best.

KEY TAKEAWAY

5. Building a Values-Driven Culture

Building a values-driven culture starts with leaders who embody and consistently demonstrate their values. They act as role models, showcasing how the organization's values can guide behavior and decision-making. Through their actions and words, leaders communicate the importance of values and set the tone for the entire organization.

Leaders also need to clearly articulate the organization's values and ensure they are well understood by all team members. This includes providing examples of how the values translate into everyday actions and behaviors. By making values tangible and relatable, leaders make it easier for team members to embrace and internalize them.

Creating a values-driven culture also involves integrating the values into various aspects of the organization, such as hiring processes, performance evaluations, and decision-making frameworks. Leaders ensure that values are considered in the recruitment and selection of team members, as well as in the assessment of performance and behavior.

Leaders must consistently reinforce the values through ongoing communication, recognition, and celebration. They highlight examples of individuals or teams who embody the values and showcase how their actions have contributed to the organization's success. This reinforcement helps embed the values in the organizational DNA and encourages others to follow suit.

In addition, leaders foster open dialogue and encourage team members to voice their opinions and perspectives. This inclusiveness allows for a diversity of thoughts and ideas, ensuring that the values are continually examined, refined, and adapted as needed.

KEY TAKEAWAY

Leaders who prioritize values create a culture where team members feel connected, engaged, and motivated. They establish a strong sense of purpose and identity within the organization, attracting and retaining individuals who share the same values. By nurturing a values-driven culture, leaders create an environment that promotes ethical behavior, collaboration, and a commitment to excellence.

6. Navigating Ethical Dilemmas

Leaders with clear values find it easier to navigate challenging situations and ethical dilemmas. When faced with complex decisions, having a well-defined set of values provides a moral compass that guides their actions and choices. Here are a few reasons why clear values empower leaders in navigating ethical complexities:

Decision-making framework: Clear values serve as a decision-making framework that helps leaders evaluate different options and determine the most ethical course of action. When faced with dilemmas, leaders can refer back to their values to ensure their decisions align with their principles.

Consistency: Clear values promote consistency in decision-making. Leaders with well-defined values are more likely to make consistent choices, even when facing difficult trade-offs or external pressures. They prioritize ethical considerations over short-term gains, maintaining their integrity and the trust of their stakeholders.

Stakeholder alignment: Leaders with clear values can effectively communicate their ethical principles to their teams and stakeholders. This alignment creates a shared understanding of the organization's values and fosters a culture of ethical behavior. It helps build trust and credibility, both internally and externally.

Role modeling: Leaders act as role models for their teams. When leaders embody and uphold clear values, they set an example for others to follow. This inspires and motivates employees to make principled choices in their own work, creating a positive ethical culture within the organization.

Long-term perspective: Clear values enable leaders to take a long-term perspective when making decisions. They consider the potential consequences and impact of their choices beyond immediate gains or losses. This helps them navigate complexities with a broader vision and ensures their decisions contribute to the long-term success and sustainability of the organization.

Leaders with clear values are better equipped to navigate ethical dilemmas and challenging situations. Their values provide a moral compass, decision-making framework, consistency, stakeholder alignment, and a long-term perspective. By prioritizing ethical considerations, these leaders can make principled choices even when faced with difficult trade-offs, ultimately earning the trust and respect of their teams and stakeholders.

KEY
TAKEAWAY

Summary

Clear values are a fundamental aspect of effective leadership. When leaders have a deep understanding of their values, decision-making becomes simpler and more aligned with their principles. Values provide a guiding framework that streamlines choices, strengthens authenticity, and builds a values-driven culture. Leaders who embody clear values navigate ethical dilemmas with integrity and inspire others to make choices aligned with shared principles. By embracing and consistently living their values, leaders create an environment of trust, purpose, and ethical decision-making, ultimately driving organizational success.

Leadership
KEY C❶NCEPTS

20

Your Personality Creates Your Personal Reality
Leaders Create the Life They Love With Passion and on Purpose

Introduction

The concept of "Your Personality Creates Your Personal Reality" suggests that our individual personalities play a significant role in shaping the reality we experience. We will take this idea further by exploring how leaders, through their unique personalities, can create a life they love with passion and on purpose. It delves into the ways in which leaders' personalities influence their mindset, actions, and outcomes, ultimately shaping their personal reality.

1. The Power of Passion:

Passion is a remarkable force that ignites leaders' souls, propelling them towards their goals and aspirations. It is the inner flame that fuels their intense enthusiasm and commitment to their vision. Passionate leaders are driven by an unwavering belief in their purpose and a deep desire to make a meaningful impact.

One of the defining characteristics of passionate leaders is their relentless pursuit of excellence. They are not content with mediocrity but strive for greatness in everything they do.

This passion pushes them to continuously seek improvement, challenge the status quo, and push beyond their limits. It drives them to invest their time, energy, and resources into mastering their craft and becoming the best version of themselves.

Passionate leaders possess an infectious energy that inspires and motivates others. Their enthusiasm is palpable, and it creates a ripple effect within their teams and organizations. By radiating passion, they cultivate an environment where creativity, innovation, and collaboration thrive. Their unwavering belief in their vision is contagious, attracting like-minded individuals who share their passion and are eager to contribute to its realization.

In the face of obstacles and setbacks, passionate leaders demonstrate remarkable determination and resilience. They refuse to be deterred by challenges but view them as opportunities for growth and learning. Their passion fuels their perseverance, allowing them to weather storms and push through adversity. They are willing to put in the extra effort, go the extra mile, and make the necessary sacrifices to overcome obstacles and continue moving forward.

Passionate leaders also have the ability to inspire others to embrace their own passions. Through their authentic expression of passion, they create a safe and supportive space for their team members to discover and pursue their own interests and aspirations. They encourage others to find their purpose and create a life they love, fostering a culture of passion and fulfillment.

Passion is not confined to a particular domain or endeavor. Passionate leaders infuse their personal and professional lives with purpose and enthusiasm. They understand that true fulfillment comes from aligning their passions with their work, relationships, and personal pursuits. This holistic approach enables them to create a life they love in its entirety, where every aspect is infused with passion and purpose.

KEY TAKEAWAY

Passion is a powerful force that drives leaders to pursue their goals, overcome challenges, and create a life they love. It propels them forward, fuels their determination, and inspires those around them. Passionate leaders are driven by an unwavering belief in their purpose and a deep desire to make a meaningful impact. By embracing their passion, they create a personal reality filled with purpose, fulfillment, and the joy of living a life driven by what truly inspires them.

2. Purposeful Vision

Leaders with a purposeful vision possess a deep understanding of their values, passions, and aspirations. Their personality traits, such as conscientiousness and goal-orientation, play a crucial role in shaping their clarity of purpose and their ability to translate it into action. Here's how purposeful vision influences leaders' personal reality:

Clear Direction: Leaders with a purposeful vision have a clear sense of direction in life. They have a compelling idea of what they want to achieve and the impact they want to make. This clarity enables them to set meaningful goals and make decisions that align with their vision. Their purpose serves as a compass, guiding their actions and ensuring that they stay on track towards creating the reality they desire.

Alignment of Values and Passions: Purposeful leaders align their values and passions with their vision. They understand the importance of pursuing goals that are in harmony with their core beliefs and what brings them joy and fulfillment. This alignment provides a strong foundation for their actions and decisions, ensuring that they are driven by a deep sense of authenticity and purpose.

Motivation and Resilience: Leaders with a purposeful vision are highly motivated to work towards their goals. Their vision acts as a source of inspiration, fuelling their determination and resilience. In the face of challenges and setbacks, they are driven by their purpose, which helps them bounce back, persevere, and continue making progress. This motivation and resilience contribute to shaping their personal reality by allowing them to overcome obstacles and stay committed to their vision.

Meaningful Decision-Making: Purposeful leaders make decisions based on their vision and values. They consider the long-term impact of their choices and prioritize actions that align with their purpose. By making decisions in line with their purposeful vision, they shape their personal reality in a way that is meaningful and in accordance with their desired outcomes.

Attracting Alignment: Leaders with a purposeful vision attract individuals who share their values and resonate with their vision. This alignment creates a positive environment where like-minded people come together, collaborate, and support one another in achieving their shared goals. By attracting individuals who align with their purpose, leaders create a network that strengthens their personal reality and amplifies their impact.

Fulfillment and Satisfaction: Having a purposeful vision brings a sense of fulfillment and satisfaction to leaders' lives. They experience a deep sense of meaning and purpose in their work and personal endeavors. This fulfillment positively impacts their personal reality, contributing to a greater sense of well-being, joy, and overall life satisfaction.

KEY TAKEAWAY

Leaders with a purposeful vision have a clear direction and a deep understanding of their values and passions. By aligning their actions and decisions with their purpose, they shape their personal reality in a way that is meaningful and fulfilling. Their purpose serves as a guiding force, motivating them to overcome challenges, attract like-minded individuals, and create a life that is in harmony with their vision.

3. Self-Confidence and Resilience

Self-confidence and resilience are key attributes that empower leaders to shape their personal reality. These traits enable leaders to navigate challenges, take risks, and embrace opportunities. Let's delve deeper into how self-confidence and resilience contribute to leaders' ability to shape their personal reality:

Belief in Abilities: Leaders with self-confidence possess a strong belief in their abilities and strengths. They have a deep understanding of their skills, knowledge, and experiences, which enables them to approach situations with a sense of assurance and certainty. This self-belief instills confidence in their decision-making and actions, empowering them to pursue their goals and aspirations.

Risk-Taking and Embracing Challenges: Self-confident leaders are more willing to take risks and step outside their comfort zones. They recognize that growth and progress often come from venturing into the unknown and embracing challenges. By having faith in their abilities, they are more likely to seize opportunities, push their boundaries, and explore new possibilities. This willingness to face challenges head-on contributes to shaping their personal reality by expanding their horizons and opening doors to new experiences.

Persistence and Perseverance: Resilient leaders possess the ability to bounce back from failures, setbacks, and obstacles. They view setbacks as opportunities for growth and learning rather than as permanent roadblocks. Instead of giving up in the face of adversity, they persist and persevere. Their resilience allows them to maintain focus on their goals, overcome obstacles, and ultimately shape their personal reality through their ability to adapt and overcome challenges.

Learning and Growth Mindset: Self-confident and resilient leaders have a growth mindset. They view failures and setbacks as learning opportunities and catalysts for improvement. They actively seek feedback, embrace constructive criticism, and continuously seek opportunities to develop their skills and knowledge. This commitment to learning and growth contributes to shaping their personal reality by enhancing their capabilities and allowing them to constantly evolve and adapt.

Inspiring Others: Self-confident and resilient leaders serve as role models for their teams and organizations. Their unwavering belief in themselves and their ability to overcome challenges inspires and motivates others. By leading with confidence and resilience, they create an environment that encourages their team members to believe in themselves and their potential. Through their example, they shape a collective reality where individuals are empowered to take risks, embrace challenges, and persist in the pursuit of their goals.

> *Self-confidence and resilience are essential attributes that empower leaders to shape their personal reality. By believing in their abilities, taking risks, embracing challenges, persisting in the face of adversity, and fostering a growth mindset, leaders can navigate obstacles and pursue their aspirations with determination and resilience. Through their actions and mindset, they create a personal reality filled with growth, success, and fulfillment, inspiring those around them to do the same.*

KEY
TAKEAWAY

4. Influential Mindset

The mindset of a leader plays a crucial role in shaping their personal reality and ultimately influences their ability to lead effectively. A growth mindset, characterized by a belief in the potential for growth and development, is particularly influential in driving positive outcomes.

Leaders with a growth mindset perceive challenges as opportunities rather than obstacles. Instead of being discouraged by setbacks, they view them as temporary and solvable. They see setbacks as valuable learning experiences that provide insights and feedback for improvement. This mindset enables leaders to maintain a positive outlook and a sense of resilience in the face of adversity.

Leaders with an influential mindset embrace continuous learning and improvement. They seek out opportunities to expand their knowledge and skills, whether through formal education, seeking feedback from others, or engaging in self-reflection. They understand that personal and professional development is an ongoing process and are committed to continually evolving and adapting.

By cultivating an influential mindset, leaders create a positive and empowering personal reality. They inspire and motivate others by demonstrating their own growth and development. This mindset encourages a culture of learning and innovation within their teams or organizations, as individuals feel empowered to take risks, learn from failures, and contribute their unique perspectives.

Leaders with an influential mindset foster a supportive environment that values growth and development. They encourage and provide resources for their team members to enhance their skills and knowledge. This promotes a sense of trust, engagement, and commitment among team members, ultimately leading to increased productivity and success.

KEY TAKEAWAY

Leaders with a growth mindset shape their personal reality by perceiving challenges as opportunities, viewing setbacks as temporary, and embracing continuous learning and improvement. By cultivating an influential mindset, leaders create a positive and empowering environment that fosters personal and professional development for themselves and those they lead.

5. Authentic Leadership

Authentic leadership is a powerful approach that emphasizes leaders being true to themselves and aligning their actions with their core values, beliefs, and strengths. By embracing their authentic selves, leaders create a personal reality that is genuine and resonates with others.

Authentic leaders are aware of their values and beliefs and make decisions that are consistent with them. They do not compromise their principles or pretend to be someone they are not. This authenticity attracts like-minded individuals who share similar values and beliefs, creating a sense of connection and trust within their teams and communities.

When leaders are authentic, they foster an environment where open communication and collaboration thrive. Team members feel comfortable expressing their ideas and concerns, knowing that their leader values authenticity and appreciates diverse perspectives. This leads to increased engagement, creativity, and innovation within the team.

Authentic leaders also inspire others by being transparent about their strengths and weaknesses. They acknowledge their limitations and seek support when needed, which promotes a culture of mutual support and growth. This vulnerability encourages team members to embrace their own strengths and weaknesses, fostering an atmosphere of continuous learning and personal development.

By leading authentically, leaders contribute to their overall life satisfaction. When leaders are true to themselves, they experience a sense of fulfillment and alignment between their personal and professional lives. This authenticity extends beyond their professional role and positively impacts their relationships, well-being, and overall happiness.

> *Authentic leadership involves embracing one's true self and aligning actions with core values, beliefs, and strengths. By leading authentically, leaders create an environment that encourages growth, collaboration, and success. They attract like-minded individuals, build trust, and contribute to their own life satisfaction and the well-being of those they lead.*

KEY
TAKEAWAY

6. Impact and Legacy

leaders who create a life they love with passion and purpose often strive to make a lasting impact on the world around them. Their strong sense of purpose and commitment to their values drive them to contribute positively to their organizations, communities, and society as a whole. By aligning their actions with their deeply held beliefs and aspirations, these leaders are able to shape a personal reality that leaves a meaningful and enduring legacy for others to follow.

Inspiring Others: Leaders who are passionate about their work and live with purpose have a natural ability to inspire those around them. Their enthusiasm, dedication, and clear sense of direction can motivate others to pursue their own passions and goals. Through their actions, they serve as role models, demonstrating the power of living authentically and following one's calling.

Creating Positive Change: Leaders who are driven by their values and purpose often seek to create positive change in their organizations and communities. They actively identify areas for improvement, implement innovative solutions, and champion causes that align with their vision. By addressing societal challenges or transforming their organizations, these leaders leave a lasting impact that improves the lives of others.

Empowering Others: Leaders who create a life they love often understand the importance of empowering others. They recognize and nurture the talents and potential of those around them, fostering a culture of growth and development. By empowering others, they create a ripple effect, as their team members go on to achieve their own successes and make their own contributions.

Building a Sustainable Future: Leaders who live with passion and purpose often have a broader perspective on their impact. They consider the long-term consequences of their actions and strive to build a sustainable future. Whether it's through advocating for environmental stewardship, promoting social responsibility, or driving ethical business practices, these leaders leave a legacy that prioritizes the well-being of future generations.

Inspiring a Legacy Mindset: One of the most significant legacies of leaders who create a life they love is their ability to inspire a legacy mindset in others. By demonstrating the power of aligning one's actions with values and purpose, they encourage others to reflect on their own lives and strive for greater meaning and impact. These leaders inspire individuals to consider how they can make a positive difference and leave their mark on the world.

Leaders who create a life they love with passion and on purpose leave a lasting impact by inspiring others, creating positive change, empowering individuals, building a sustainable future, and instilling a legacy mindset. Their actions and contributions serve as guiding lights for others, enabling them to shape their own meaningful legacies and contribute positively to the world.

**KEY
TAKEAWAY**

Summary

Leaders with unique personalities have the power to shape their personal reality by creating a life they love with passion and on purpose. Their passion, purposeful vision, self-confidence, resilience, influential mindset, and authentic leadership contribute to their ability to shape their personal reality. By embracing their individuality, leveraging their strengths, and aligning their actions with their values and purpose, leaders pave the way for a fulfilling and impactful life. Understanding the influence of personality in shaping personal reality empowers leaders to live authentically, pursue their passions, and inspire others to do the same, ultimately creating a world where individuals can thrive and make a difference.

Leadership
KEY CNCEPTS

Strive To Do Your Best
Leaders Dont Let Perfect Get in the Way of Good

Introduction

In the pursuit of excellence and success, leaders often face the challenge of balancing the desire for perfection with the need for progress. While striving for perfection can be admirable, it can also hinder productivity and impede decision-making. Effective leaders understand that perfection is elusive and that progress is more important than achieving an unattainable ideal. We will explore the importance of striving to do one's best while not letting perfectionism hinder progress and growth.

1. The Pursuit of Excellence

In the realm of leadership, the pursuit of excellence is a driving force that propels individuals and teams towards achieving exceptional results. Effective leaders understand the importance of striving to do their best and instill this mindset within their teams. By setting high standards, encouraging continuous improvement, and fostering a culture of excellence, leaders inspire their teams to reach new heights of success. This paper explores the significance of the pursuit of excellence in leadership and its impact on creating a culture of continuous improvement.

Setting High Standards: Leaders who strive to do their best set high standards for themselves and their teams. They establish clear expectations and communicate their vision for excellence. By setting the bar high, leaders challenge their teams to push beyond their comfort zones and reach for greatness. High standards provide a sense of direction and purpose, guiding individuals and teams towards achieving exceptional outcomes.

Encouraging Continuous Improvement: Striving to do one's best involves a commitment to continuous improvement. Effective leaders foster a culture where learning, growth, and development are valued. They encourage their teams to seek opportunities for self-reflection, feedback, and skill enhancement. By promoting a growth mindset and providing resources for development, leaders create an environment that supports the ongoing pursuit of excellence.

Embracing Innovation and Creativity: Leaders who strive to do their best recognize the importance of innovation and creativity in achieving excellence. They encourage their teams to think outside the box, explore new ideas, and challenge conventional wisdom. By fostering an environment that embraces innovation, leaders inspire their teams to find creative solutions, break through barriers, and achieve exceptional results.

Leading by Example: Leaders who strive to do their best lead by example. They demonstrate a strong work ethic, a commitment to excellence, and a drive for continuous improvement. By embodying the values and behaviors they expect from their teams, leaders inspire and motivate others to follow suit. Leading by example establishes a standard of excellence and creates a culture where individuals are inspired to give their best.

Recognizing and Celebrating Achievements: Leaders who strive to do their best recognize and celebrate achievements along the way. They understand the importance of acknowledging the efforts and accomplishments of their teams. By celebrating milestones and recognizing exceptional performance, leaders inspire a sense of pride, motivation, and camaraderie. This recognition reinforces the value of striving for excellence and encourages individuals to continue giving their best.

Cultivating a Growth Mindset: Leaders who strive to do their best cultivate a growth mindset within their teams. They encourage a positive attitude towards challenges, failures, and setbacks. By promoting a belief in the power of effort, resilience, and continuous learning, leaders create an environment that fosters personal and professional growth. A growth mindset empowers individuals to embrace challenges, overcome obstacles, and constantly improve their performance.

The pursuit of excellence is a fundamental characteristic of effective leadership. Leaders who strive to do their best set high standards, encourage continuous improvement, and cultivate a culture of excellence. By leading by example, embracing innovation, recognizing achievements, and fostering a growth mindset, leaders inspire their teams to reach for greatness. The pursuit of excellence creates a sense of purpose, drives continuous improvement, and propels individuals and teams towards achieving exceptional outcomes.

KEY TAKEAWAY

2. The Perfectionism Trap

While perfectionism may initially appear as a positive trait, it can become a trap that hinders both leaders and their teams. Here are some ways in which the pursuit of perfection can have negative consequences:

Unrealistic Expectations: Perfectionistic leaders tend to set extremely high standards for themselves and others. While aiming for excellence can be admirable, an excessive focus on perfection can lead to unrealistic expectations. This can create immense pressure and stress, potentially leading to burnout and decreased productivity.

Analysis Paralysis: Perfectionism often manifests as an obsession with getting every detail absolutely right. This fixation on perfection can lead to over-analyzing and indecisiveness, known as analysis paralysis. Leaders caught in this trap may spend excessive amounts of time and energy seeking the "perfect" solution, causing delays in decision-making and hindering progress.

Fear of Failure: Perfectionistic leaders often have an intense fear of failure. They may view any form of mistake or imperfection as a personal flaw or a reflection of their competence. This fear can create a risk-averse environment where innovation and creativity are stifled. Team members may feel hesitant to take risks or propose new ideas, fearing potential criticism or falling short of unrealistic standards.

Diminished Team Morale: The relentless pursuit of perfection can lead to an environment where mistakes are heavily criticized and discouraged. This can negatively impact team morale, as individuals may become anxious and afraid of making errors. The fear of not meeting perfectionistic standards can dampen motivation and diminish engagement within the team, hindering collaboration and inhibiting the potential for growth and innovation.

Lack of Adaptability: Perfectionism can make it difficult for leaders and their teams to adapt to changing circumstances. The rigid focus on achieving perfection often leaves little room for flexibility and adaptation. When unexpected challenges arise, leaders may struggle to adjust their plans and strategies, leading to missed opportunities or an inability to effectively respond to new situations.

Overcoming the perfectionism trap requires leaders to cultivate a healthy balance between striving for excellence and accepting imperfections. They can:

1. Set realistic expectations and communicate them clearly to the team.

2. Foster an environment that encourages learning from mistakes and values continuous improvement rather than flawless outcomes.

3. Encourage innovation, creativity, and risk-taking by emphasizing the importance of learning through experimentation and embracing failure as a stepping stone to success.

4. Cultivate a supportive and collaborative team culture that celebrates progress and effort rather than solely focusing on perfect results.

5. Practice self-compassion and encourage team members to do the same, recognizing that mistakes are a natural part of the growth process.

KEY TAKEAWAY

Leaders allow team members to thrive, contribute their unique perspectives, and collectively work towards achieving shared goals. By recognizing and addressing the potential pitfalls of perfectionism, leaders can create an environment that promotes growth, creativity, and resilience, enabling both themselves and their teams to thrive.

3. Embracing Progress Over Perfection

Embracing progress over perfection is a mindset that can greatly benefit leaders and their teams. Rather than striving for an unattainable level of perfection, effective leaders understand that progress and continuous improvement are key to success.

Leaders who prioritize progress recognize that perfection can often be an unrealistic and paralyzing goal. Perfectionism can lead to excessive self-criticism, fear of failure, and a reluctance to take risks. By shifting the focus to progress, leaders create an environment that encourages experimentation, innovation, and learning from mistakes.

Leaders who embrace progress understand that small steps forward are significant and valuable. They break down larger goals into manageable tasks and celebrate each milestone achieved along the way. This approach not only maintains momentum but also boosts morale and motivation within their teams.

By valuing the process of growth, leaders encourage a culture of continuous improvement. They foster an environment where team members are encouraged to try new ideas, learn from failures, and adapt strategies as needed. This mindset of progress creates a sense of psychological safety, where individuals feel empowered to take initiative and contribute their best efforts.

Leaders who embrace progress understand the concept of "good enough." They recognize that in certain situations, seeking perfection can be inefficient and time-consuming. Instead, they encourage their teams to focus on delivering high-quality results within reasonable timeframes. This approach allows for flexibility, adaptability, and the ability to iterate and refine as necessary.

Embracing progress over perfection also allows leaders to maintain a sense of balance and well-being. It helps prevent burnout by avoiding the unrealistic pressure to achieve flawless outcomes. By acknowledging that progress is a continuous journey, leaders can celebrate achievements along the way and find fulfillment in the process of growth.

Leaders who prioritize progress over perfection understand the limitations of perfectionism and the benefits of continuous improvement. By valuing incremental progress, embracing the concept of "good enough," and fostering a culture of learning, leaders create an environment that encourages innovation, resilience, and long-term success.

4. Taking Calculated Risks

Taking calculated risks is an essential quality of effective leaders. They understand that progress and growth often require stepping outside of comfort zones and exploring new opportunities. By embracing a mindset of experimentation and learning, leaders create an environment where taking risks is encouraged and valued.

Leaders who take calculated risks understand the importance of weighing potential benefits against potential risks. They conduct thorough research, analyze available data, and consider various scenarios before making decisions. While they recognize that risks are inherent in any endeavor, they strive to minimize potential negative outcomes and maximize the likelihood of success.

By encouraging their teams to take risks, leaders foster a culture of innovation and growth. They understand that failure is not necessarily a negative outcome but rather an opportunity for learning and improvement. When teams are empowered to take risks, they become more willing to think creatively, explore new ideas, and challenge the status quo. This mindset fosters innovation and can lead to breakthroughs and competitive advantages.

Leaders who value calculated risks also create an environment that supports learning from failures. When setbacks occur, they encourage their teams to analyze what went wrong, extract valuable lessons, and apply those insights to future endeavors. This iterative process of learning and adapting allows teams to continuously improve and refine their approach.

Leaders who embrace calculated risks set an example for their teams. They demonstrate courage, resilience, and a willingness to step outside their own comfort zones. This inspires others to overcome their fears and embrace new challenges, fostering a culture of personal and professional growth.

It's important to note that taking calculated risks does not imply reckless decision-making. Effective leaders consider the potential impact on stakeholders, the organization, and the team members. They balance ambition with careful evaluation and consideration, ensuring that the potential benefits outweigh the potential risks.

Leaders who are willing to take calculated risks create an environment that encourages innovation, growth, and learning. By embracing experimentation and learning from failures, they foster a culture where continuous improvement is valued. By setting an example and empowering their teams, leaders inspire others to step outside their comfort zones, leading to increased creativity, productivity, and success.

KEY TAKEAWAY

5. Empowering Others

Empowering others is a crucial aspect of effective leadership. Leaders who prioritize progress over perfection understand the importance of creating an environment where team members feel empowered to take ownership, contribute their ideas, and take on new challenges.

By empowering their team members, leaders foster a sense of autonomy and ownership. They provide individuals with the necessary resources, support, and guidance to excel in their roles. Rather than micromanaging or imposing rigid processes, they encourage team members to think independently, make decisions, and take initiative. This autonomy and trust build confidence and motivation within the team.

Leaders who prioritize progress also create a culture where individuals feel safe to contribute their ideas and perspectives. They value diversity of thought and actively seek input from their team members. By creating an open and inclusive environment, leaders encourage creativity, innovation, and collaboration. They recognize that great ideas can come from anywhere within the team and are willing to listen and learn from others.

Leaders who prioritize progress understand that mistakes and failures are part of the learning process. They create an environment where team members feel safe to take calculated risks and learn from setbacks. Rather than penalizing mistakes, they view them as opportunities for growth and development. They provide constructive feedback and support to help individuals learn from their experiences and improve their performance.

By empowering others, leaders foster a sense of ownership and accountability. When individuals feel empowered, they are more likely to take pride in their work and go the extra mile to achieve excellence. They become more engaged, motivated, and committed to the team's goals.

KEY TAKEAWAY

Leaders who prioritize progress over perfection empower their team members by providing autonomy, fostering a culture of inclusion and innovation, and embracing the learning process. By creating an environment where individuals feel safe to contribute and take risks, leaders inspire their teams to strive for excellence, leading to increased motivation, engagement, and overall success.

6. Celebrating Achievements

Recognizing and celebrating achievements is an essential aspect of effective leadership. It serves multiple purposes, including boosting morale, fostering a positive work environment, and motivating individuals and teams to continue performing at their best. Here are a few reasons why celebrating achievements is crucial:

Encourages a positive work culture: Celebrating achievements helps create a positive work environment where individuals feel appreciated and valued. It cultivates a sense of camaraderie, teamwork, and support, which can lead to increased job satisfaction and employee engagement.

Motivates and inspires: Recognizing achievements and milestones provides motivation for individuals and teams to continue working hard and strive for excellence. Celebrating successes serves as a reminder of the progress made and reinforces the idea that hard work pays off.

Reinforces desired behavior: By acknowledging and celebrating achievements, leaders reinforce the behaviors and actions that contributed to success. This recognition helps individuals understand what actions are valued and encourages them to continue their efforts in that direction.

Boosts morale and confidence: Celebrating achievements boosts morale by providing a sense of accomplishment and pride in one's work. It enhances confidence and self-esteem, which can positively impact future performance and encourage individuals to set even higher goals.

Enhances retention and loyalty: Recognizing and celebrating achievements contributes to employee satisfaction and loyalty. When individuals feel appreciated and recognized for their hard work, they are more likely to remain committed to the organization and contribute to its long-term success.

Sparks innovation and continuous improvement: Celebrating achievements creates a culture of innovation and continuous improvement. It encourages individuals and teams to share their success stories, exchange ideas, and learn from each other's accomplishments, leading to further growth and progress.

To effectively celebrate achievements, leaders can use various methods such as public recognition, team events or outings, awards, certificates, or personalized tokens of appreciation. The key is to tailor the celebration to the individual or team and make it meaningful and sincere.

> *Celebrating achievements is an integral part of effective leadership. By recognizing and appreciating the efforts and accomplishments of individuals and teams, leaders inspire motivation, boost morale, and foster a positive work environment, ultimately contributing to continued progress and success.*

KEY TAKEAWAY

Summary

Effective leaders strive to do their best while recognizing that perfection is not always attainable or necessary. They understand the importance of progress, continuous improvement, and taking calculated risks. By embracing progress over perfection, leaders foster a culture of growth, innovation, and empowerment. They inspire their teams to embrace the learning process, take ownership, and celebrate achievements along the journey toward excellence.